J.COM

THE CORRECT LINE?

Uganda under Museveni

Olive Kobusingye

authorHOUSE®

AuthorHouse™ UK Ltd.
500 Avebury Boulevard
Central Milton Keynes, MK9 2BE
www.authorhouse.co.uk
Phone: 08001974150

First published by AuthorHouse   9/15/2010

ISBN: 978-1-4520-3962-6 (sc)

Cover photograph by James Akena: March 2010, General President Yoweri Museveni visiting Bududa, Eastern Uganda, the site of massive landslides that buried three villages, leaving close to four hundred people dead and more than five thousand others homeless.

This book is printed on acid-free paper.

In memory of my younger brother, Saasi, and in honour of those Ugandans who died while fighting for fundamental change.

Acknowledgements

I express my sincere gratitude to the men and women who shared the stories of their lives with me, some at the risk of attracting unfavorable attention from the state. I am grateful to the many people who shared their views and thoughts with me through interviews and who, in so doing, helped me to crystallise my own thoughts about Uganda. I thank Sam Mugumya for research assistance, Wycliff Bakandonda for help with locating information, and Mohammed Mbabazi for access to the Uganda On-line Law Library. I am deeply indebted to Frederick Golooba-Mutebi and David Sseppuuya, whose help with the preparation of the manuscript was truly invaluable. In a very special way I acknowledge the infinite support of my family. In addition to keeping me focused on the story, my husband has been the wind beneath my wings, and he and our girls have put up with my long absences even when I was in the house.

Abbreviations

CA	Constituent Assembly
CBS	Central Broadcasting Services
CMI	Chieftaincy of Military Intelligence
COS	Chief of Staff
CPS	Central Police Station
DISO	District Internal Security Officer
DP	Democratic Party
EC	Electoral Commission
ESO	External Security Organisation
FDC	Forum for Democratic Change
IDP(s)	Internally Displaced Person(s)
ISO	Internal Security Organisation
LDU	Local Defence Unit
LRA	Lord's Resistance Army
MP	Member of Parliament
NRA	National Resistance Army
NRM	National Resistance Movement
PGB	Presidential Guard Brigade
PPU	Presidential Protection Unit
RA	Reform Agenda
RDC	Resident District Commissioner
UPC	Uganda People's Congress
UPDF	Uganda People's Defence Forces
USh	Uganda shillings
UTV	Uganda Television
WBS	Wavah Broadcasting Services

Contents

Preface

One afternoon in 1981, when I had been at Makerere University for only a couple of weeks, my niece Annette burst into my room at Africa Hall wailing. Her mother, Beatrice Kemigisha, had just been taken by Obote's security operatives. A lecturer at the university, Beatrice had been picked up from her office, driven home, and roughed up while her captors ransacked the house. She was then driven away. We never saw her again. This event marked my personal introduction to the politics of struggle and terror in Uganda.

In 1986 when I was preparing to write my final exams in medicine, the National Resistance Army (NRA) stormed Kampala and took over power. The five years between those two events were characterized by terror, both distant and up close. At the height of the Luwero bush war, we often arrived at the hospital in the morning to find Red Cross trucks offloading their cargo of the injured and dying from the war zone. In the night we went to sleep to the sound of screaming from Old Mulago village, where residents were regularly robbed, raped, and harassed. I can remember very distinctly the feeling of terror that gripped us whenever we met soldiers in the valley between Makerere Hill and Mulago on our way back from the medical school. One never knew how that encounter might end. The pounding heart, the dry mouth, the sickening feeling as the stomach bottomed out and your legs nearly gave way under you. And the sense of immense relief once you walked through the gate into the campus, having survived. These are experiences that I will never forget.

Towards the end of the war, it seemed that each time we ventured out we were taking our lives into our hands – simply to do things that should have been routine, like going to school or to the shops. Any time the alarm might be sounded: '*Bazze! Bazze!*' 'They've come! They've come!' We all knew the rebel army was coming, but we also knew that they would not take over the city without the government forces putting up a fight, so everyone dreaded being caught in the wrong place in that final showdown. That day in 1986, after a long and dreadful night, morning had come. The sun was shining. The shadows vanished. Things looked very rosy indeed.

On that day over twenty years ago, Ugandans were like George Orwell's characters in *Animal Farm* on the morning after they liberated themselves from the tyranny of Mr. Jones:

> remembering the glorious thing that had happened they all raced out into the pasture together.... The animals rushed to the top of it and gazed round them in the clear morning light. Yes, it was theirs – everything that they could see was theirs! In the ecstasy of that thought they gambolled round and round, they hurled themselves in the air in great leaps of excitement.[1]

In January 1986 there was every reason for most Ugandans to believe that the bad times were gone forever. Everyone's aspirations were right there, well articulated in the new government's ten-point programme. Now a quarter century later, the near unanimity of euphoria with which Ugandans celebrated the arrival of the National Resistance Army has turned to disillusionment.

This book tells the stories of some of those Ugandans whose experiences over the last two and a half decades contrast sharply with what was expected in that 'new' Uganda. It tells some of the stories that are unlikely to be told by the government's salaried writers, whose only perspective of Uganda seems to be that of peace, prosperity, and galloping development. The book has its roots in the many conversations that I have had with people all over the country in markets, hospital corridors, offices, outside police stations and court

---

1   George Orwell, *Animal Farm* (London, England: Penguin Books Ltd, 1987 edition).

rooms – people whose lives were being lived out in circumstances radically different from those depicted by the regime's enthusiasts. It became clear to me that their stories were an important and valid part of our history. To deny them would be to deny a part of what Uganda is. To acknowledge them would hopefully cause us and our children to question more earnestly those leaders that offer to liberate us and that offer to sacrifice themselves for our salvation / while holding us and our thoughts hostage to personal visions that only they understand. For some liberators it must be quite confusing to transition from the mode where you kill your enemies to one where you respect your opponents and treat them with civility. Plotting the best way to kill one's enemies (the essence of war) is perhaps not good preparation for governing a country in which some people – or indeed many people – disagree with you most strongly and say so with annoying frequency. The mustard seed does not germinate and grow into a mango tree.

It is ironic that the National Resistance Movement party chose a bus for its symbol. A bus is normally driven by one driver. There is not much teamwork involved in driving a bus; it is perfectly normal for a bus driver to function without consulting those seated on the bus. The passengers trust that the driver knows the route. They get on the bus, find a seat, get comfortable, and either read the daily newspaper or watch the scenery go by the window. In Uganda people on buses easily get into conversation though they might be perfect strangers. They might get into heated arguments about football or local politics. The bus driver ignores them, as he should, and carries on driving. The driver knows the way. But what if the driver decides to change the route? What if he or she gets lost? What if the driver falls asleep or suffers a seizure while at the wheel?

I recall one night when I was an intern doctor working in Machakos General Hospital in Kenya, the police woke up my colleagues and I to attend to the victims of a disaster. A bus with eighty passengers on board, some of whom were probably asleep at the time, had veered off Mombasa road and plunged into a river. The driver, who had no doubt driven this route countless times, had taken the lives of eighty trusting passengers and had plunged them into a river with devastating consequences. (Bus drivers can indeed get you to your destination – but they can also take you to disaster.)

This book does not attempt to give a detailed account of all that has happened in Uganda under Yoweri Kaguta Museveni's rule. Rather, it opens a window through which we can see Museveni, the man that has been at the helm of Uganda's government for the last quarter of a century. And beyond the man we should see Ugandans and what has become of their 'fundamental change' in those years. Children born the year the National Resistance Army shot its way to power have been eligible voters for years. They have gone to school, grown up, gone to work, and started families. Many who were born in the war-torn northern part of Uganda grew up in camps for the internally displaced, where indeed some started their own families, thus commencing a generation whose only world view was the camp.[2] The only president these young Ugandans – more than 50 per cent of the country's population – have ever known is Museveni, who maintains that (he does not see anybody in the entire country who has the capacity to succeed him.)Not his vice president, not the vice chairman of the ruling party (of which Museveni has been the chairman since 1985), and not any among his cabinet of more than sixty ministers. Museveni alone knows the route and how to drive the bus.

With the idealism of youth at the time the NRA came to power, we saw everything as black or white, right or wrong, true or false. We supported those we believed to be honest, and we rejected those perceived to be liars. We judged quickly and harshly. Most things had sharp edges. As we have grown older, those edges have been somewhat blunted by our own failures. We have experienced situations where there was not one truth but many, and sometimes

---

2   In August 2001 there were 480,000 internally displaced persons (IDPs) living in camps. By 2005 there were over 1.8 million, which accounted for over 90 per cent of the population in the affected region. Uganda had the notoriety of being the country with the largest number of IDPs in the world. Beginning in August 2006, when a cessation of hostilities agreement between Uganda government and the rebel Lord's Resistance Army (LRA) was signed, the camps were disbanded, and the camp residents were encouraged to 'go home' to villages the majority of them never knew before.

where there appeared to be no truth at all. We have had to choose between people and causes that are neither right nor wrong, but that are more sensitive, more practical, or more pragmatic; causes that do not necessarily promise to save the world (but that promise to improve it just a little.) We do not value honesty and integrity any less than we did then. On the contrary, we put a premium on these values, but we accept imperfection in others because we have been humbled by our own faults. In all this, though, we should be willing to acknowledge when we have been systematically and consistently cheated, lied to, and exploited. If we lose the ability to confront these unpleasant truths, the future will be lost.

Olive C. Kobusingye
August 2010

Foreword

Few studies of contemporary Ugandan political history are complete without understanding the persona of incumbent President Yoweri Kaguta Museveni. And yet surprisingly, there have been hardly any book-length analyses of the man who has ruled the country – for better or worse – for the last twenty-five years of the country's forty-eight-year history. What is perhaps even more surprising is that most of the analyses which have been written have been glowing, reverential, and largely uncritical – praising Museveni for saving a country that in the mid-1980s could have been described as the 'sick man of Africa'. In this book, Museveni the political actor is given a second look; it is an analysis that takes us beyond the many accolades he has garnered over the last two and a half decades, and it exposes the numerous limitations behind the political animal who has ruled Uganda for longer than any other leader in the country's history, pre- or post-independence.

In selecting the title *The Correct Line?* Olive Kobusingye goes to the heart of the many ironies and contradictions that characterize President Museveni and the regime of governance that was ushered into the country during the heady early days of 1986. What is correct about militarism, or about the increasing descent of what was once a popular leadership into personal rule? What is correct about the prevailing corruption, nepotism, and electoral gerrymandering, all of which were ailments that forced Museveni to take up arms in 1980 – and which he so stridently criticized when he assumed power? What could have been an ideological clarion call for genuine and fundamental change in the country (the correct line) is demonstrated to be little more than a homogenizing mantra designed to stifle debate and suppress organized opposition. Criticism of the correct

7

line is only tolerable in certain spaces: hidden from public view, couched in obscure language, and where the blame is ultimately placed elsewhere than where it really belongs. Were he to look in the mirror today, Museveni would see only a slightly modified version of Uganda as it was in 1980.

But the strength of Kobusingye's book lies not so much in the deep political and historical analysis, at which it excels. Rather, it lies in the personal juxtaposition of her own story against that of Museveni's and Uganda's. For Kobusingye was a Museveni fellow-traveller and early convert to the ideals of the Movement system of governance that became the hallmark of the fundamental change that was ostensibly represented by the rise to power of the NRA/M. Coming of age just as the NRA/M entered Kampala, Kobusingye could be described as a Movement cadre – if not in practice, at a minimum in belief and support for the regime. In this respect, *The Correct Line?* is the story of so many Ugandans who have lived through the same period; it is a story of renewed hope dashed by growing disbelief and crowned by searing betrayal.

Even more tellingly, Kobusingye is sibling to Dr. Warren Kizza Besigye, political nemesis and arch-rival to Museveni in the previous two presidential elections of 2001 and 2006, Besigye is scheduled – all things being equal – to size up against him again in 2011. Although some of Kobusingye's perspectives may be coloured by this filial connection, it is nevertheless a unique point of view which provides insights about a disillusioned disciple in a political system gone awry. But from the vantage point of having been in the trenches in both campaigns, through accounts of disappearances, detentions, and even deaths, Kobusingye's *The Correct Line?* exposes the soft underbelly of the Museveni regime in a manner that no journalistic or academic account has ever done. And there lies the rub: while the Museveni regime has profoundly transformed the economy and political discourse in the country, it has done so in a deeply Machiavellian fashion. Hence, the Museveni government has incarcerated more journalists than those detained in all of Uganda's previous regimes; it has overseen numerous deaths in custody and has established an elaborate system of illegal and punitive detention-without-trial through the so-called safe houses. *The Correct Line?* does not flinch from exposing these stories. More chilling, many of them are drawn from first-hand accounts, demonstrating in graphic and convincing fashion how the Museveni 'revolution' has devoured so many of its own children.

J. Oloka-Onyango
Professor of Law, Makerere University

Chapter 1: Picking a Leader of Somebody Else's Choice

'Get down!' the policeman yelled at me, his voice both urgent and hushed. And in a desperate whisper, he added,: 'Take off the T-shirt and cap!' I dropped to the ground and tried to pull off the campaign T-shirt without raising my arms to where they might be seen above the low partition that separated the bank veranda from the street. The cap was easy to discard. I now had my face a couple of inches from the policeman's boots and was doing my best to remain invisible to anybody walking on the street.

Through a slit between the policeman's legs and the edge of the divider, I could see soldiers of the Presidential Protection Unit (PPU) dragging people, mostly young men, out of alleys and hitting them like robbers. Among the victims were two girls; the soldiers pounced on them with their boots and gun butts. The youths were unarmed, and many had thrown off their Kizza Besigye campaign T-shirts, leaving their bare backs even more vulnerable to the beatings. They protested their innocence, but to no avail. Some were kicked and told to get out of town, while the less fortunate were marched off to some unknown fate. After a while – probably only fifteen to twenty minutes of mayhem – a sudden and dreadful silence fell over the town.

The date was 3 March 2001, and this was in the south-western town of Rukungiri at the height of the presidential campaigns of that year. Only less than an hour before, Dr. Kizza Besigye had addressed a mammoth rally in the town sports grounds. It was the first rally I had attended. The announcement of Besigye's candidature and his instant popularity with a large section of the population had taken the country by storm, with his rallies causing waves of excitement all over the country. The evening before the rally, my sister Margaret and I had set off from Kampala at around 6.00 PM. Our plan was to do the six hours or so to Rukungiri in a straight shot. But just as we approached Mbarara, some two hours away from home, with Margaret half asleep at the wheel from accumulated exhaustion, we pulled in for the night at one of the local hotels. At dawn we set off and got into Rukungiri just as the town was coming to life. Everyone was relieved that we had decided not to stick to the original idea of travelling at night because, unknown to us, there had been shootings targeted at Besigye and his supporters. Had we shown up then, we might have been prime targets.

All the apprehension was pushed to the side on the morning of the big rally as the excitement over the day's activities reached fever pitch. The whole town was buzzing – throngs of people in Besigye T-shirts and caps, cars decorated with posters, songs, whistles… everywhere the optimism was palpable.

Besigye had planned to address rallies all over the district counties, culminating in a final megarally in the town of Rukungiri. We travelled from one frenzied rally to the next all morning and part of the afternoon. Everywhere we stopped, we were met by hundreds, and at times thousands, of people. They chanted campaign songs and were so excited at the prospect, and what seemed like the very real possibility, of a change in government that it must have been frightening for those still campaigning for Museveni. This went on through all the counties we stopped in, until we started turning full circle towards Rukungiri. It became very difficult to move at a reasonable pace because of the throngs of people pouring onto the road and blocking the motorcade. It was impossible to make only scheduled stops. In any event, we kept pushing on until we arrived back in Rukungiri amidst an overwhelming emotional welcome; there was hardly any standing space in the streets. We were told that some of the people had walked for hours; others had come the previous day to be sure that they would be present at this historic rally.

The atmosphere was electric, and everywhere people kept saying in a matter-of-fact fashion that Museveni had no chance at all. The rally was going to be addressed by all the opposition heavyweights:

Sam Njuba, Winnie Babihuga, Atanasio Rutaro, Prince Vincent Kimera, and Nassar Ntege Sebaggala. Many of Sebaggala's 'boys'[3] had come down to Rukungiri the day before and were now going up and down the streets singing campaign victory songs and waving Besigye pictures. Other groups had come to town as well, most notably Makerere University students in the main from Rukungiri and the neighbouring districts of Bushenyi and Ntungamo. They carried huge banners declaring 'Makerere for Besigye' and 'Besigye for President'. These students would later be targeted and summarily beaten by the military. Some would flee for their lives on foot, walking for up to ten miles to escape their assailants. A driver would manage to get away with a bus on four wheels, but with not a single glass or light left intact. But that was later.

Shortly after Besigye's motorcade got back into town, as if on cue, Sebaggala and the rest of the opposition leaders came in from the other end of the town, to another tumultuous welcome by the huge crowds. When Sebaggala stood up to wave to the crowds, the noise was deafening. However, unnoticed or simply ignored by the majority of the people in the crowd, a sinister pattern was forming on the fringes of this jubilant scene. As we would later learn, the Museveni camp had allegedly planned to disrupt the rally and, having failed to keep away the people, had eventually decided that they would strike terror when all were gathered in the sports ground.

But for the moment, the rally got started and the speakers did not disappoint. The line-up had been carefully selected, and each speaker spoke with the kind of passion and conviction that could only come from long suffering and the unshakable belief that freedom and victory were clearly in sight. All the speeches were relatively short and to the point: enough was enough; Museveni had squandered

---

3   Nassar Ntege Sebaggala had a huge following among the young and especially among the unemployed or underemployed, popularly called 'Seya'. He first gained notoriety when he was arrested in the United States of America for attempting to transact business using fake travellers' cheques. After a jail sentence that he served in a Boston prison, he returned to a hero's welcome and went on to win the election for Kampala city mayor. After his bid for president hit a dead end for lack of the requisite academic qualifications, he gave his support to the Elect Kizza Besigye camp.

the good will of the people and had abused their trust, and it was now time to show him the exit. Each speaker was welcomed with thunderous applause. When Besigye took to the microphone to address the rally, the crowd went completely wild for several minutes. When Besigye eventually managed to get started, it was as though his listeners held their breath to catch every word. Although the grounds must have held upward of a few thousand people, every word could be clearly heard.

Besigye warned that because of the insecurity caused by the Museveni forces, the rally would be kept short so that people could go back to their homes in safety before nightfall. Unlike many of the speeches that Besigye had given during the campaign, some of which aimed to inform, educate, and convince, this one simply affirmed a position already held by the masses themselves. Everyone, he counselled, should go out on polling day to participate in the overdue act of sending Museveni into retirement. And almost too soon for an event that had been anticipated for weeks, the rally came to an end. The presidential candidate and his entourage left amidst as much excitement as there had been on their arrival, and the people started milling around—some singing and chanting, others chatting and analyzing the events of the day. The young people who had marched through the streets before the rally resumed their parade, now even more energized. Most had their hands in the air flashing the two-finger sign for the Reform Agenda (RA).[4] Some carried Besigye pictures, and others blew whistles as they marched.

Not being one to join such a march, I found my way towards the periphery of the action and spotted Winnie Babihuga's pick-up truck parked outside the Commercial Bank building.[5] I went over and was beginning to talk to the driver when suddenly, amidst the

---

4   During the 2001 campaigns, the term Reform Agenda was loosely used to describe those who were pushing for political reforms and supporting the candidacy of Dr. Kizza Besigye. The organisation was at that point called the Elect Kizza Besigye Taskforce. Reform Agenda was formally constituted in July 2002.

5   Winnie Babihuga was a member of the 6th Parliament (1996–2001). She left active politics after 2001 following a much-contested parliamentary election in which Winnie Matsiko was declared winner. She currently works for the United Nations.

jubilation, there erupted a spate of rapid gunfire. In the space of a few seconds, the shooting was repeated and was even more sustained. I fell to the ground, half rolling and half running toward the bank building. There was screaming everywhere. Terrified people were running for their lives, mostly heading away from the town centre. Gunshots seemed to come from everywhere. Shop fronts that had been open only minutes before were now firmly locked. Together with the driver and the youth who had been aboard the pick-up truck, I was caught with no cover. Had it not been for the quick thinking of a policeman guarding the bank, I might have been one of those at the receiving end of the Presidential Protection Unit's physical assault. The sounds and the sights of the day stayed with me for a long time.

For several minutes after the guns fell silent, nobody dared to move. Then slowly and tentatively, doors began to crack open. People who had ducked into unfamiliar doorways started to get out. The policeman, seeing that things were calm again, told me to get away from the bank and find a safer place to hide. Unsteadily, I got onto my feet and, after looking around to see if indeed I could leave without attracting attention, joined the small stream of terrified people leaving the town. We had all witnessed such extreme and unwarranted brutality that for a while nobody said anything. What could anyone say?

As we put a safe distance between ourselves and the scene of the horror, people began to talk. We were all relieved to be alive, but everyone knew of other people who had been at the rally, and we all had our fears about where they might now be. The following day we learned that one man, forty-seven-year-old Johnson Baronda, had been gunned down by the PPU. Unofficial reports said three people had been killed, but these were never confirmed. The shooting injured many, but they were probably so happy to be alive that they said nothing further about the incident. The two girls I had seen being battered showed up the following day, all bumps and bruises and hardly able to walk. This incident of premeditated state terror on unarmed and nonviolent civilians was not the first that had taken place during that campaign. For me, it was nevertheless the first close encounter. Captain Atwooki Ndahura and the PPU soldiers under his command who perpetrated this violence were never apprehended for these crimes. Indeed, Ndahura was promoted to Lieutenant Colonel and in 2010 was decorated with the Luwero Triangle Medal.

Chapter 2: A Troubled Past

'If a government does not bother to solve the problems of its people,
what does it expect? Does it expect peace?' – Yoweri Museveni[6]

The story of postcolonial Uganda is one of bloody wars and ugly
dictatorships. The irony is that unlike many countries in Africa, which
came to independence through armed struggle, Uganda's transition
from British rule to self-government in 1962 was relatively peaceful.
That peace was short lived. The 1962 constitution gave Buganda
kingdom a federal status within Uganda. It also recognized four other
monarchies as having semifederal status, including Ankole, Toro,
Bunyoro, and the territory of Busoga. The Kabaka (king) of Buganda,
Sir Edward Mutesa, became the first head of state. The relationship
between Mutesa and his premier was difficult, characterized by
mutual mistrust and intrigue. In 1966 Milton Obote, then Prime
Minister, ordered the army to attack the Kabaka's palace, and in
the ensuing violence the Kabaka fled into exile. As the dictatorship
matured, all those that had alternative views risked imprisonment or
worse. Obote used all means to get rid of opposition, and in 1969 he
declared Uganda a one-party state.

In his book *Sowing the Mustard Seed*, Museveni noted of this period,
'Many prominent Ugandans were subjected to detention without
trial, that hallmark of Africa's political underdevelopment.' On the
attack of the Kabaka's palace specifically, Museveni commented thus:
'During the 1966 crisis when Obote was quarrelling with Mutesa,
Obote's army massacred many people. If Mutesa is having a political
quarrel with Obote, what does the population have to do with it
and why kill them? I do not agree with the proverb that when two

6   Yoweri Museveni, 'Building Uganda for the Future', *What Is Africa's
Problem?* (University of Minnesota Press, 2000).

elephants fight, it is the grass that suffers. If people are rioting you can arrest them and put them in prison. The government has a lot of power to deal with rioting people and means to control crowds without killing them.'[7]

In September 2009, Museveni's government would be given the opportunity to put this conviction to the test in response to Museveni's disagreement with the Buganda king, Kabaka Muwenda Mutebi. The armed forces moved in and shot dead at least twenty-seven civilians in Kampala, some of who were reportedly dragged from behind the closed doors of their homes.

Courtesy *New Vision*

In September 2009 spontaneous demonstrations broke out in Kampala and several towns in the Buganda region. This followed a decision by the Uganda government to bar the Buganda king, Kabaka Muwenda Mutebi, from travelling to Kayunga, a part of his kingdom. The security forces massacred at least twenty-seven civilians during the riots on 10–11 September.

---

7   Yoweri Museveni, 'The Price of Bad Leadership', *What Is Africa's Problem?* (University of Minnesota Press, 2000).

In 1971 Obote was in turn overthrown by his army commander Idi Amin. After a long and expensive war that used Tanzania as a base, Amin was eventually overthrown in 1979 through the joint effort of the Tanzanian army and a number of Ugandan armed groups. It is estimated that as many as a half a million Ugandans were killed during Amin's eight year dictatorship. Amin's exit saw Obote return to the country, and after a couple of short-lived governments led by Professor Yusuf Lule and Godfrey Binaisa and a Presidential Commission, Obote returned to the helm. In 1980 Ugandans had a chance to turn a clean page by electing leaders of their choice – and the rigging of those elections in Obote's favour triggered Museveni and his colleagues to wage yet another war to rid the country of a leadership that they said did not have the mandate of the people.

The 1980 elections were plagued by a host of irregularities. Voter registration started on 6 October 1980 and lasted a little over two weeks – hardly enough time, considering the state of insecurity and limited mobility in some parts of the country. In fact, in West Nile and parts of the northern districts, registration did not happen at all. Where it did take place, there were complaints that names were added or deleted from the registers after the exercise had ended. The registers were displayed briefly – and in some places not at all. The nomination of candidates was a fiasco – in many places, notably in the north and in Kasese, DP candidates were either detained on nomination day until the end of the voting exercise, or their nominations were cancelled afterwards. Two days before the polls, the Electoral Commission announced that votes would be transported to a central, 'safer' place where the counting would be done the following day. This announcement caused consternation among non-UPC circles because it contradicted an earlier agreement with the parties that the votes be counted at the polling stations right after the close of the poll. The polls took place on 10 December 1980, and the Military Commission announced the results two days later. Any credibility that the elections might have had evaporated after the tallying process and declaration of results were hijacked from the electoral commission and rested solely in the hands of Paulo Muwanga, the Chairman of the Military Commission. Under this atmosphere of uncertainty, suspicion, and a sense of powerlessness among the people, UPC was proclaimed the winner. The elections were witnessed by an observer group from the Commonwealth Secretariat at the invitation of the Ugandan government. A summary of their report read thus:

> This has been a turbulent and troubled election, characterized by confusion, delays, intense mistrust, and in the end a sense of wonder that it happened at all.
>
> Some, at least, of the difficulties could have [been] mitigated, even in Uganda's situation, if the Electoral Commission had been a more efficient and imaginative body than proved to be the case; if the Military Commission had not delayed a final decision and announcement on the venue and manner of the count till just three days before polling; ... if logistical arrangements for distribution of balloting material had been made with a greater deal of thoroughness.
>
> Surmounting all obstacles, the people of Uganda, like some great wave, carried the electoral process to a worthy and valid conclusion.[8]

Less than two months after that, Museveni launched the bush war that would usher him into State House five years later.

Early on in the war, Museveni explained why he and his group chose to fight and why they expected to win the war:

> We are fighting a just cause. We are fighting for the democratic rights and human dignity of our people, all of which have been trampled on by Obote and his erstwhile protégé Amin for nearly two decades. Our women shall no longer be raped by bandit soldiers; our citizens shall not be robbed or beaten at road blocks; nobody, not even a tramp on the road, shall be killed unless so condemned by the courts. Court orders shall be obeyed by even the highest government officials;

---

8   'Report of the Commonwealth Observers Group 16/12/1980', Parliament of Uganda Archives.

elections shall take place and they shall not be rigged; the right to be treated with respect and courtesy by these so-called officials, the right to life, the right to dignity, are not favours to be bestowed by anybody. They belong to our people by right.[9]

Ugandans would have ample opportunity to test out this pledge with Museveni at the helm.

---

9   Yoweri Museveni, *Selected Articles on the Uganda Resistance War* (1985).

Chapter 3: Rocking the Boat

'Our mandate was a limited one: to fight to restore freedom, by which we meant that the people should be given the chance to decide on their destiny, without manipulation.' – Yoweri Museveni[10]

One evening in late October 2000, my sister Margaret called me to her house in Ntinda, a Kampala suburb. She said it was urgent. Considering I had talked to her earlier in the day and there had been nothing unusual, I was somewhat surprised. She said she was not free to talk about it on the phone, so I drove to her house to find my younger brother Saasi's car already in the driveway. My other sister, Stella, arrived shortly after. Margaret said that Besigye had called his siblings to the impromptu meeting and that he was on his way. It was approaching nine o'clock when he eventually showed up. Only my third brother, James, was absent. After brief pleasantries Besigye apologized for getting us to drive to Ntinda in the night and for keeping us waiting, but he said a situation had arisen that made it imperative that he talk to us as a matter of urgency. Now he had all our attention. 'I know some of you are not interested in politics,' he started, 'but you are now about to be engaged in it, probably against your will.' He then told us that he had been in extensive consultations with some of his friends and colleagues, many of them in government, and that they had come to a decision that he should run against Museveni for president in the coming elections.

For several moments the announcement sort of hung in the air as we all kept quiet. Only Margaret did not look surprised. I did not know what to think. This was all too sudden, too unexpected. I had been

---

10   Yoweri Kaguta Museveni, 'Fighting Obote', *Sowing the Mustard Seed* (London & Basingstoke: Macmillan Publishers Ltd, 1997).

aware for sometime that my brother had fallen out with the centre of the Movement government, but I had not expected that this might be the result. Then Besigye continued. 'The formal announcement will come out in the press tonight, so I did not want you to be surprised. I also wanted to warn you that from now on you are probably going to be dragged into discussions you would rather stay out of, and you can expect a lot of inconveniences. I hate to bring this upon you, but my colleagues and I have come to believe that it is inevitable.' He went on to explain that if the opportunity of the coming elections was not seized, and if Museveni carried on unchallenged, then the country risked sliding back to the same mess that they had gone to the bush to resolve. A short discussion followed, with questions and explanations going back and forth. Besigye repeated his warning that we might be targeted for harassment, and I recall Margaret saying she was not going into a second exile. After a while Besigye said he had yet another meeting to get to, so we wished him Godspeed and dispersed. On my way home, I saw the early version of the *New Vision* newspaper on the street, and sure enough the news of Besigye's candidacy was right there on the front page. I think that in some definitive way that was the beginning of my private and reserved brother becoming public property. Whereas in his earlier days in the Movement government he had served in public roles, he was now leaping from the seemingly calm waters of the lagoon to the open and stormy sea. It remained to be seen which of his friends and colleagues would join him and how the political landscape would change as a result of that rift.

Back in late 1986 when the NRA was still new in town, I had left the country to do my internship in Kenya. When I returned I spent some three months at Besigye's house. It was an unusual household. There was a constant flow of visitors: diplomats and herdsmen, soldiers of all ranks (and some of no ranks at all), old women that called Besigye their son, and young men that called him their brother, but I did not know them. In the four years that he had spent in the bush war, my brother seemed to have acquired more relatives than all of the ones we had before the war. Some I can remember vividly because they became my relatives too. There was an old man from Ngoma called Bagarukayo. He was probably in his late sixties, with grown sons that became my brothers and a relatively young and beautiful wife. Mzee Bagarukayo was diagnosed with prostate cancer, and he stayed in Mulago Hospital for many months. Besigye spent hours at his bedside. When he died some announcements said that Besigye's father had died. Bagarukayo's son John stayed in Besigye's home until he was ready to go to college. Then there was Malita, better known as Commander Malita or Mama Chama. Malita was no ordinary old woman – she was an institution. She commandeered vehicles and drivers in order to visit her other children. It seemed that all the NRA senior officers had adopted her as their mother. Today she might go to Salim Saleh's house, tomorrow to Mugume's or Tinyefuza's, and the following week to see Mzee (Museveni). Malita brought many of her extended family (*abantu bange*) with her. I do not know if all those other homes where she went housed as many of Malita's people as Besigye's did. She got a house of her own in Old Kampala but was still mostly to be found at one of her sons' homes. Through Malita I also acquired another brother called Kangave. Then there were the soldiers and drivers. They were mostly young men with not too much education. They shared a special bond with Besigye. There never seemed to be any doubt in their minds that Besigye had their best interests at heart and that their future was secure in Mzee's hands. It was from those soldiers that I first heard the expression, '*Mzee anapanga*' – Swahili for 'The old man [Museveni] has plans for us'.

There was Sekyanzi, who was a bit of a clown and a ladies' man. There was rather shy Segirinya, the driver, and he always drove like the devil was after him. There was Olena, who I believe came from somewhere in Teso; he spoke good English and decent Luganda. Then there was Rugunju, who lived in the staff quarters with his wife. The wife seemed to have some special status among the household workers. When Rugunju fell ill and finally died, he was mourned and missed like a close relative.

Mealtimes at Besigye's house were interesting affairs. One never knew if there were going to be eight people or eighteen. When more people came, the cook quickly watered down the sauce and made more *kawunga* (maize meal).

I soon moved out of this lively establishment to my own apartment, and I started life as a busy surgical resident. What I recall from those months is the way all those people who had been in the bush war related to one another. It was clear that Besigye considered his newly acquired relatives just as important as his blood relatives. If he made a commitment to help someone, he would be willing to die trying to fulfil the promise. I was often roped in to resolve health care–related commitments. But underlying everything was frugality and an almost religious commitment to watching out for everyone's good. There were few luxuries, but the soldiers accepted that things were tight everywhere and that when the situation improved, everyone would be better off. It was a couple of years later, while I was away again (this time at the University of London), that I first heard that Besigye seemed to be in trouble with the establishment. He had been 'reassigned', but in effect he was being stripped of key leadership responsibilities. Evidently, the trend did not stop.

While for most people Besigye's troubles appear to have started in 1999 with the writing of the controversial article criticising the Movement (see document in annex), this was the culmination of a long drawn-out disagreement that had been kept out of public view.

In the Constituent Assembly (CA) in 1994 as one of the ten army representatives, Besigye had argued, together with fellow officers David Tinyefuza and Serwanga Lwanga, that the NRM should be considered a transitional arrangement and that the ban on political parties should be lifted before the 1996 elections. This minority position was rejected by the Constituent Assembly.

Pointing to the efforts made by Besigye and other military officers who made serious attempts to bring about reform in the governance structures, Mugisha Muntu recalled, 'They were the same people that brought up these issues over and over. But once Museveni discovered that it was the same people – a small group that could be ignored, that might not influence the situation – he did nothing. We thought that it was possible to build a critical mass so that they can tip the balance. That is what made some of us to leave – because it had become apparent that that critical mass was only possible outside the power structure… all those years we thought it was possible to do it from within. There was always that hope.'

Chapter 4: All Ugandans Are in the Movement

'A system can appear to be free, but you find that in essence, it is not so. For instance, you can manipulate the ignorance of the people and make them make decisions that will militate against their interests. Can this be called freedom? Can freedom include manipulation? Should there be freedom to manipulate, misinform, and take advantage of people's ignorance? Is that democracy? I personally do not think it is.' – Yoweri Museveni[11]

The 2001 presidential campaign was conducted under very unusual circumstances. Political parties were still banned, and candidates were supposed to be nominated on the basis of 'individual merit.' All candidates, and indeed all citizens, were by legal compulsion members of the Movement, which was said not to be a political party. When Besigye declared his intentions to run for president, that should have been perfectly in order – but it was not. Museveni, who had clearly expected to be the only candidate not linked to one of the old parties, found this candidacy to be most objectionable. In 1996 Paul Kawanga Ssemogerere's bid for the presidency was informally supported by a coalition of political groups that favoured political pluralism. Because UPC was part of the coalition, the Movement was able to link Ssemogere to past discredited regimes under which the country had come to ruin. Many had also seen him as an opportunist that served under any government that offered him a ministerial position. This was not going to work with Besigye, who had no links to previous regimes and who could lay claim to

---

11   Yoweri K. Museveni, 'Political Substance and Political Form', *What Is Africa's problem?* (Minnesota University Press, 2000).

the achievements of the National Resistance Movement so far. To cut him off from any support that he could have counted on from the Movement, Museveni declared that Besigye had deserted the Movement. To make that point, Museveni surrounded himself with his cabinet in a clear bid to demonstrate that only he enjoyed their unwavering support. At times as many as six cabinet ministers would appear with Museveni on a television programme, prompting the joke that the president was moving around with a cabinet choir to sing his praises. But if there had been subtle cracks in the Movement fabric before, the campaign drove deep pegs into those cracks, and the chances of healing receded with every passing week.

On 25 November 2000, Museveni was declared the 'only candidate' for the Movement by the Parliamentary Caucus. In the Movement Caucus the members resolved:

> – That we welcome the recent announcement by President Museveni that he will offer himself again for election
>
> – That we endorse the candidature of Y. K. Museveni as the torch bearer of the Movement in the said presidential elections
>
> – That we bind ourselves to fully support and advance the candidature of Y. K. Museveni to victory by mobilizing all people in our constituencies to give unconditional support to him.[12]

This resolution, formally penned on 9 December 2000, was duly signed by the Parliamentary Caucus Chairman, Professor Gilbert Bukenya. At the time, contradictions were mounting rapidly. The Movement was an all-inclusive 'no party', yet it was fielding a presidential candidate and implying that only that candidate was eligible to stand on its ticket. If all Ugandans were indeed in the Movement, this meant that no other Ugandan was expected to run for the presidency. In addition, it had not been possible for the (banned) political parties to send their representatives to Parliament. This was

12   *Monitor*, 25 November 2000.

because all those in Parliament were by compulsion members of the all-inclusive Movement and had been elected on the basis of their individual (personal) merit, not as flag bearers of any party. After Dr. Kizza Besigye launched his campaign, however, an NRM caucus was formed. The dishonesty in the NRM's stance on party politics was exposed by Human Rights Watch:

> Only one political organization in Uganda is exempted from the strict regulations placed on political activity in Uganda: the ruling National Resistance Movement (NRM). The NRM has effectively excluded itself from regulation by characterizing itself not as a political party but as a 'movement,' fusing its structures with those of the Ugandan state, and creating a pyramid of 'movement' structures from the village level to the national level. All Ugandans belong to the 'movement,' even those who oppose it: compulsory membership that is itself inconsistent with the right *not* to be forced to belong to an association. The 'movement' structures are state-funded and are administered at the national level by a National Political Commissar, who is responsible for the political mobilization and education of the population. By denying that the NRM is a political party, the NRM avoids being forced to comply with the regulations imposed on opposition political parties, and by fusing its structures with the Ugandan state the NRM gains direct access to state funds and the powers of state mobilization. Since the NRM is not officially a political party, despite having the characteristics of a ruling political party in a single-party state, it has sought to create the illusion that Uganda is a 'no-party' state. Such semantics obscure the basic reality of the NRM's partisan dominance of the political process in Uganda.[13]

13   *Human Rights Watch*. Hostile to Democracy: The Movement System and Political Repression in Uganda, (New York: Human Rights Watch 1999), http://www.hrw.org/legacy/reports/1999/uganda/.

This apparent injustice was not lost on the various groups and parties that were opposed to the Movement. For those who advocated for the lifting of the ban on political parties, the battle lines were clear. However, there was inertia and confusion among those who had been strong supporters of the Movement but were now feeling disenfranchised. Museveni was not unaware of these sentiments. Long before serious and overt rifts occurred in the Movement structures, he had sought to distinguish Uganda's political arrangement from a ruling one-party system. While addressing the African Caribbean and Pacific nations/European Economic Community Joint Assembly in Kampala in February 1991, Museveni had tried to distinguish the two:

> There is also another distortion in politics by those who run one-party systems. If I express an opinion that you do not like and you expel me from the party but do not allow me to form another one, then I am effectively disenfranchised. This practice has created a lot of problems in Africa.... We do not expel members from the Movement: if you must expel people, logically, you must allow them to form another party.

In 1991 nobody was publicly contesting for the leadership of the mass movement that Museveni had founded, so there was no need to 'expel' anyone. In 2000, however, these assurances evaporated with Besigye's challenge for the presidency. Anne Mugisha described how the mirage of the all-inclusive Movement started to vanish:

> After Besigye got locked out of the Movement's National Executive Conference, it became clear that there was no internal democracy, that this was a one-party state, and that what we had mistaken for national structures were actually party structures. So we were orphaned. It was like a carpet being pulled from under our feet. We had built structures thinking they were national, but one party now owned them. We were outside of the party, and with no structures whatsoever. This was the anomaly that Ruranga

Rubaramira was trying to correct when he petitioned to stop the local council elections, because Museveni was using national structures as party structures.[14] I recall Ofwono Opondo[15] [NRM spokesperson] once asking, 'You people – we have the RC system, how do you think you are going to win this election?'[16]

Anne Mugisha joined politics as an activist in November 2000 to support the Elect Kizza Besigye Task Force. She had worked as a career Diplomat in the Ministry of Foreign Affairs and as an Information Officer in the Ministry of Finance. She went into exile in August 2001 but is an active member of the Forum for Democratic Change (FDC), the largest opposition political party.

David Mpanga, an Oxford University–trained barrister who had just returned to Uganda, and whose mother was a Member of Parliament, thought the whole system was a fraud:

> I had a problem with the idea that everybody was in the Movement, but someone could cross to the Movement. Then where were they before? If you determine that everything that exists – all matter – is in the universe, then how can anybody be outside the Universe? If you have now come into the Universe,

---

14   Constitutional Petition Number 21 of 2006, *Rubaramira Ruranga versus the Electoral Commission and the Attorney General*. The petition successfully challenged the constitutionality of certain provisions of the Local Governments Act (LGA), the National Women's Council Act (NWCA), the National Youth Council Act (NYCA), and the regulations made under these acts. http://www. kituochakatiba.co.ug/Judgment%20Rubaramira%20Ruranga.pdf (accessed 15 October 2009).

15   Opondo, a journalist, underwent a Saul-to-Paul conversion in 2000, from being a fierce NRM critic to one of its most ardent defenders, and later the party's Deputy Spokesperson. In 2005 he suffered public ridicule after the *Monitor* newspaper reported that he had been arrested for shoplifting underwear at a Kampala supermarket. He sued the paper but changed his mind and dropped the case.

16   The RC, or Resistance Council, was the system on which the Movement was organized. It had state-funded structures from the national level down to the villages. Resistance Councils were renamed Local Councils in the 1995 constitution.

where were you before? I was of the view that the lie about the all-inclusive nature of the Movement, even if it might have been necessary at one point, was responsible for a number of the problems coming up at the time. They were propagating one lie which required that they then tell many other lies to cover up. My problem at the time was the fusion of the state with the party. For instance the use of the Movement facilities – I would say, 'if we are all in the Movement, then why can't we all use the Movement Secretariat?' And someone would say, 'Oh – but you are not in the Movement!' So if the Movement embraced everyone, why was it not churning out everybody's ideas, views, and materials, why was it focusing on the views and interests of one group – or one man? Why was the army still an extension of one party? Why were some military people openly partisan, making it clear they wanted one particular candidate to win?[17]

Tall and impeccably dressed, with his tie perfectly knotted and centred, Mpanga looked every inch the image of a young, successful city lawyer. His boyish, almost mischievous smile gave the impression that every legal battle was a welcome challenge, much in the way dedicated chess players approach a contest with a titled opponent they have not had the pleasure to play against. His Oxford English rolled off with ease and without the comical forced accents so common among some of Kampala's foreign-trained professionals.

In some ways Mpanga was a rather unlikely source of sharp criticism for the Movement. His mother was very involved with the formation of the NRM and, before that, had been one of the promoters of Museveni's Uganda Patriotic Movement in the 1980 elections.

My mother served in clandestine roles in Kampala during the bush war, so we were all very sensitized about governance issues. Right through Idi Amin and Obote, we were told, and could see for ourselves, that these were bad regimes. We were also told the

17   Interview with David Mpanga, December 2009

NRA/NRM stood for the forces of good. During the [bush] war many people that I now know to have been involved in the war effort came through our home – Sam Katabarwa, my uncle Kanyerezi, I later came to understand about their involvement in these activities – such as fund raising, and helping to smuggle people who were involved in the struggle.

So when the NRM came to power there was a lot of jubilation. As an undergraduate student in England I had a picture of Museveni on my wall. I even took on a kind of 'left-of-centre' approach to life. So I was very supportive of the regime.[18]

On the same day that the Movement Caucus bound itself 'unconditionally' to Museveni's presidential bid, Brig. Henry Tumukunde[19] and his wife arrived in Rukungiri in style – aboard a military helicopter, no doubt fuelled and paid for by the people's taxes, to attend a private marriage ceremony – at which he was reported to have said that he would not salute any other head of state but Museveni. At another meeting in Bushenyi, then Minister Miria

18   Interview with David Mpanga. Mpanga's father was the Attorney General of Buganda when Kabaka Mutesa's palace was invaded by Obote's soldiers in 1966. His mother, Joyce Mpanga, was the first woman in Uganda's Legislative Council (LegCo) and has remained politically active since then. His grandparents and great grandparents on both sides of the family had been politically active in Buganda. Three generations of political activism were unlikely to leave Mpanga indifferent to governance.

19   Tumukunde is a lawyer and bush war veteran that sustained a firearm injury to his hip during combat, leaving him with a subtle limp. He is married to Janet Museveni's niece. Among the many high-profile jobs he has held are Chief of the paramilitary Internal Security Organization (ISO) and Army Representative in Parliament. Before that he was Division Commander in Gulu, northern Uganda, and was later charged with putting names of nonexistent soldiers on the army payroll and pocketing their salaries. In 2005 he fell out with Museveni after making statements critical of the president during a radio program. In May 2005 he was ordered to resign his parliamentary seat and was later arrested and charged in the Military Court Martial with 'spreading harmful propaganda' and insubordination. He was kept under some form of house arrest, which was flexible enough to allow him travel to the United States on family business.

Matembe[20] likened all those challenging Museveni in the election to frogs wallowing in the mud. She said any Ugandan who did not vote for Museveni was like the biblical Israelites who abandoned God after he had miraculously redeemed them from the hand of the Egyptians. (From being a strong Movement and Museveni supporter, Matembe has become one of their most ferocious critics, especially regarding the government's poor record on fighting corruption. In 2005 she was dropped from cabinet after she opposed the lifting of presidential term limits.)

As the campaign picked momentum, so too did the acrimony between the candidates, and the suffering and persecution of those in the de facto opposition. The Movement seemed to be afflicted by the same malady that had bothered the UPC three decades earlier, as Museveni so aptly noted: 'Incapable of practicing democracy within itself, the UPC could hardly have expected to nurture it in the country at large.'[21]

---

20   Miria Matembe is a lawyer. She was Minister of Ethics and Integrity (1998–2003) and spearheaded the formulation of the government's policy on corruption. She also served as a member of the Pan-African Parliament, where she chaired the Committee on Rules. In 2002, she published a memoir entitled *Gender, Politics and Constitution Making in Uganda*. She was instrumental in negotiating a constitutionally mandated quota of at least 29 per cent women in the national Parliament. She gained early notoriety when she proposed that men who are convicted of rape should be castrated.

21   Yoweri Kaguta Museveni ,'A Brief Historical Review', *Sowing the Mustard Seed* (London & Basingstoke: Macmillan Publishers Ltd, 1997).

Chapter 5: Crisis of Identity, Crisis of Conscience

'I have used up one of the two terms provided for in the 1995 Constitution and as you have asked me, and since it is also my conviction that there is some work not complete, I am willing to present myself as one of the candidates in the coming elections for two reasons: ... The issue is that the army is not developed professionally. I cannot walk away if the army is not stable.... I think I am the one who can attend to the army because there is no corner of the army I do not know.

'We must have orderly succession. I will not be party to disorderly succession. We shall win as we have always done. After, we shall all sit under a cool atmosphere and deliberate on who can fit in the shoes of this man.' – Yoweri Museveni[22]

Picture the village elders' council. The village chief has grown old and frail. He can no longer lead the warriors into war. He can no longer sit for entire afternoons to arbitrate in the land wrangles among his people. The time has come for the elders to sit under the big tree to choose the man (yes, it has to be a man) most suitable to take the mantle.

Now picture a country of close to thirty million people. The country has an executive, a legislature, a judiciary, and a constitution. Between the constitution and the Presidential Elections Act, there is a comprehensive prescription on how succession should happen. So why is the president worried about disorderly succession? Or the size of his shoes?

---

22   Part of acceptance speech on nomination for candidacy. *Monitor*, 27 November 2000.

Many in the opposition, particularly those who had belonged to the Uganda People's Congress (UPC)[23] and Democratic Party (DP)[24], had expressed scepticism about the honesty of the Movement, and of Museveni in particular, way before 1996. During the 1996 presidential election, there had been corroborated reports of electoral malpractice by state organs and individuals in government in favour of the incumbent. In some districts, including Rukungiri, Museveni supporters had threatened to beat up opposition candidate Paul Ssemogerere and had denied him and his entourage opportunities to address the people. Oloka-Onyango, a professor of law at Makerere University, pointed to the dishonesty of the Movement system in the lead-up to the election.

> The real character of the RCs [Resistance Councils] as a grassroots mechanism for the consolidation of movement rule emerged in the 1996 elections, dispelling any notion that they were truly participatory or that they could be genuinely non-partisan. Despite the fact that the elections were held on the basis of individual merit, the state's power and resources were manifest in aiding some candidates and in intimidating others, especially those with known multiparty sympathies.… The situation was made worse by the NRM's blatant intimidation of Ssemogerere and his supporters. Furthermore, the NRM harassed opposition political actors into breaking ranks and joining the NRM. During the election, such chicanery was combined with the heavy deployment of state resources and institutions in favour of incumbent Museveni.[25]

Those who had observed the 1994 Constituent Assembly (CA) elections were not surprised:

23   UPC was largely discredited due to the gross mismanagement of the country in all spheres, particularly in Obote's second term (1981–1985).
24   DP, believed to have won the 1980 general election, was cheated of that victory and has never been in power.
25   J. Oloka-Onyango, 'Uganda's "Benevolent" Dictatorship', 30 August 1998. http://www.hartford-hwp.com/archives/36/503.html

The 1994 CA elections marked the beginning of the monetisation of Ugandan elections: there were many cases of bribery and outright manipulation. Moreover, the electoral law allowed [Museveni] the continued use of his presidential privileges which made the 39 campaign days less problematic.... In 1995 the NRM government introduced the '*Entandikwa* Credit Scheme' as one of its poverty alleviation measures. Under the scheme, the government set up a revolving fund of 6.8 billion Uganda shillings [US$6.5 million] from which soft loans were to be given out on application. Contrary to normal banking practice the scheme was administered through the NRM political establishment. Applicants were required to apply for consideration through their Local Councils. Thus the '*Entandikwa* Credit Scheme' became an indirect method of bribing the electorate. The timing of the scheme and the manner by which it was administered exposed the political intentions behind it.[26]

Frank Atukunda, who was about to enter university in 1996, described how the campaigns went in Ntungamo district in Western Uganda.

The majority of people did not question some of the actions taken by government then, which were clearly meant to disadvantage the de facto opposition. People in government were openly partisan, and if they did not themselves engage in acts of intimidation against candidates opposed to Museveni, they certainly did nothing to discourage it. I remember bridges were destroyed on the eve of Ssemogerere's visit to the district, to bar him from coming to meet the people. Those in the opposition were hounded and taunted by government operatives, and they had no voice at all. Who could they complain to when those that were entrusted with keeping the peace were the perpetrators?[27]

26   William Muhumuza, 'Money and Power in Uganda's 1996 Elections', *African Journal of Political Science* (1997), Vol. 2 No. 1:168–179.
27   Interview with Frank Atukunda, March 2009.

Despite these blatant abuses of the electoral process, the majority of Ugandans had given the Museveni leadership the benefit of the doubt. In the lead-up to the 2001 elections, those people who had expressed doubts about Museveni's democratic fervour were vindicated. On 25 November 2000, when the resolution from the Movement's National Executive Committee concerning Museveni's sole candidacy was presented to the National Conference, the much-hailed 'individual merit' principle was found to have 'revealed some weaknesses which need to be urgently addressed before the next presidential and parliamentary election to ensure that the Movement supporters act in a harmonious and coordinated manner when choosing their political leaders'. The Movement could no longer eat their cake and have it without exposing their dishonesty – but they were still going to try.

The actions of the state grated rather loudly against the words of the key architect of the National Resistance Movement:

> There are a lot of mockeries of 'democracy' around the globe. In our case, for democracy to be meaningful and not a mockery, it must contain three elements: parliamentary democracy, popular democracy and a decent level of living for every Ugandan. In other words, there should be an elected Parliament, elected at regular intervals and such elections must be free of corruption and manipulation of the population.[28]

Election fever had turned Kampala, and indeed the whole country, upside down. It was something of a national mass hysteria. The announcement of Besigye's candidature hit the media following a drawn-out exchange between Besigye and Museveni, provoked by a document that Besigye had authored on the deteriorating quality of governance under the Movement (see annex). In the paper, which Museveni barred Parliament from discussing, Besigye had observed that the Movement had over time become undemocratic, deceitful, and opportunistic. Rather than examine the validity of these claims, Museveni had instead chosen to threaten Besigye with disciplinary action and prosecution in the military court martial. In what was

28   Yoweri Museveni, *Selected Articles on the Uganda Resistance War* (1985).

to become his signature style in dealing with dissent, Museveni, in a statement published in the local press, said, 'This is the sort of indiscipline that I am always obliged to quell using all appropriate means in the interest of our glorious army.' He came across very much as the sole authority who determined the fate of those unwise enough to cross his path.

The campaign, which would pit the two men against each other and last much longer than most people would have imagined, had commenced.

The average Kampala resident has never entered the main train station – or any train station. Passenger rail travel is practically nonexistent. The railway station building sits on a piece of prime property at the head of Nasser Road close to where it curves to join Jinja Road. The wide space defined by that curve and the adjoining Jinja Road was once a lovely park, a splash of green in the city. Overlooking the park, away from the junction of both roads, sits Crest House. This is where the Elect Kizza Besigye Task Force housed their offices in the heady campaign days of 2001. In a span of a few weeks, Crest House was transformed from a quiet office block adjacent to a sleepy train station building to a hub of frenzied activity that carried on all hours and that often spilt over into the park. Soon the park began to look like an extension of the campaign offices, with various groups having meetings there, officials addressing the press, and party enthusiasts matching up and down in preparation for rallies.

Previously unknown Louis Otika shot to prominence as the Head of Administration for the Elect Kizza Besigye Task Force. Quiet spoken and polite to a fault, Otika was a civil servant par excellence. What he lacked in innovation and speed he more than made up for in consistency and patience. In no time at all, it seemed as though every county and village in the country had an Elect Kizza Besigye campaign team, complete with an executive and offices. There were agents, mobilizers, and journalists; youth and women leaders; and representatives of all manner of special-interest groups. There were those who claimed to have highly confidential information regarding sinister plans being hatched by the Movement. Then there were those who came from the Museveni campaign team purporting to have converted into Reform Agenda supporters. It was hard to know who was genuine and who wasn't. Everyone was welcomed, even those suspected of being moles.

For the most part that was no problem because the Elect Kizza Besigye team had nothing to hide – but there were very discouraging moments when those who had been welcomed turned around and 'crossed', claiming that the Kizza Besigye camp was disorganized, or tribalistic, or undemocratic, or whichever other label they thought would do the most harm. Amanda Magambo was one such turncoat. Amanda showed such great dedication in the first few weeks of the campaign that she got elevated to the Vice Chair of the youth desk. Although some were sceptical, warning that she had close links with the Museveni camp, she seemed to be genuinely working to reach the youth and mobilize them for the Elect Kizza Besigye campaign. She was bright, attractive, and hard working – an apparent magnet for the youth. Then one morning we woke up to the disheartening news in the press that she had 'crossed' to the Museveni camp, claiming that the Besigye campaign lacked direction. Those that had suspected her of being a mole were vindicated, especially as she immediately rose through the ranks on the other side. Either she was taking what had been her rightful place all along, or she was being rewarded for her successful mission at Crest House.

Another case was Iddly Baryareeba. Iddly was a very vocal campaigner, the sort that constantly appeared on radio talk shows to make the case for the Reform Agenda. He was not famous for his diplomatic stance, and at times he seemed to go out of his way to annoy and insult Museveni's supporters. This went on for quite a while until the campaign was in its last weeks – then, with no apparent cause, Iddly crossed to the Museveni camp and became as loud and obnoxious a Reform Agenda critic as he had been a defender. People close to him said he had all along been a mole in the Reform Agenda camp – but things were moving at such a pace that it was not easy to determine just how much damage these betrayals did, if indeed that's what they were. As the RA picked momentum, the Movement became more and more aggressive in their efforts to undermine the Reformists. While they were not expected to play fair, some of what they did was outright criminal, and in fact they only got away with it because belonging to the Movement somehow elevated them above the law.

One afternoon late in the campaign, it became known that the Movement was planning to publish messages to damage the Besigye campaign in a local paper. Some had derogatory messages about the Kabaka, clearly intended to turn the Buganda Kingdom against Besigye's Reform Agenda. One purported that the RA had imported truckloads of machetes to arm their supporters countrywide, who would use these on the population in the event that they lost the election. The pull-outs with their poison messages were due to come out in the next day's *New Vision* newspaper, and because it was so close to the polls, the RA would have no time to effectively counter them. In any case, RA would be diverted from their campaign efforts and would channel their time and energy into trying to refute this baseless and senseless propaganda. The stakes were very high indeed. The *New Vision* was fully in the hands of, and at the disposal of, the Movement. RA would have to act very fast with a solid case in order to stop the release of the publications. After hasty consultations, it was decided that the best move was to ensure that the publications were stopped at the printing stage. Two Reform Agenda lawyers were dispatched to do battle. Their first stop was the Jinja Road Police station, a short distance from the *New Vision* printing premises. The lawyers lodged a complaint, the legal basis of which was that they had good information that an electoral offence was being committed or was about to be committed: publishing, or causing to be published, false or insulting information about a candidate in the election. They said they had learnt that the offence was being committed in the premises of the *New Vision* Printing and Publishing Company. If the police did not act on the information and the offence went ahead, they too would be liable. The officer in charge of the station, not wanting trouble on his hands, quickly called his superiors for advice. They in turn called the *New Vision* legal secretary, Robert Kabushenga, himself a lawyer. Within a short time Kabushenga arrived at the police station sporting shorts and sandals – obviously having dropped whatever he was doing to come and save the Movement's poisonous ads project. The three lawyers engaged in a battle of wits as the police officers stood by and watched. Kabushenga maintained that the publishing house was simply doing a job ordered by a client and that he was not free to discuss clients' businesses. It turned out that VR-Promotions was the client – the same company that was handling all the publicity for the Movement campaign. The Museveni camp had hired VR-Promotions, an advertising company, to do their dirty work. In the end, although the Besigye Taskforce was not able to legally stop the production of the offending publications, their effect was neutralized by the preemptive disclosure of the plot.

Sadly, not all missions against the Movement's dirty-trick campaigns ended so successfully. It was always frustrating to confront an incumbent that did not play by any rules, in a situation where the opposition had no recourse, because the law could not come to their rescue.

There seemed to be no limits to what could be used to discredit an opponent in the campaign. One evening a cousin called me and asked if Anselm, Besigye's son, was all right. I had seen him a couple of days before, and I said that to my knowledge he was fine. There was an uncomfortable pause, and then she told me to please check, and she hung up. I called Besigye's house and the maid answered. I could hear Anselm making noise in the background. I asked if everything was okay, and the maid assured me that they were all doing very well and that Anselm was having his dinner. The following day I discovered what this was all about. A rumour had been put out that Anselm had died and that Besigye and Winnie, his wife, were so bent on carrying on with the campaign that they had put the child's body in the mortuary and rushed back to the campaign trail. The level of malice was shocking. Apparently the story had gained such currency that Edith and Martha Byanyima, Winnie's sisters, got journalists to meet Anselm in the Sheraton gardens the following afternoon. I never learned the origin of this rumour.

If the opposition thought that the 2001 campaign was a fiasco, it was because they did not know how much worse things would become in 2006. Most of us involved in the campaign effort had never been in politics; we certainly had never run a campaign. It was mass volunteerism from the start. I did not go to the RA office very often, and the few times I went I felt somewhat lost. There were throngs of people, each one looking for someone or something to help with the campaign effort – unlike me, who would show up for a few minutes and go back to my routines in the hospital. During the polls the data centre was populated by more than fifteen dedicated people who had not been paid a cent. They were determined to stay up all night, several nights in a row, to ensure that the data from the polling stations got punched in as soon as it became available. People did not need to know anybody or need to be known – although this was to change later. Anne Mugisha had vivid memories of that heady period:

> Those early days [2001 election campaigns] were characterized by a lot of learning and discovering. I recall one time we received an invitation from the then Minister of Information, Basoga Nsadhu, to go and discuss how we [election task forces] were going to deal with the media coverage. In retrospect we realized that we were being naïve. To think that the Movement would call us to genuinely discuss how to deal with the media! With that invitation they were doing two things – they were using this to show the world that they were engaging in a democratic process, and we were helping them by making ourselves available. At the time we were not savvy enough to see and expose it for what it was – layers of deception – the deception of the internal audience, the deception of the opposition to think that the government was actually interested in a level playing field, then the international community, who would say, 'yes, Uganda is taking another leap along its democratic development path.'

> But we did not see it at the time. We played into it – and it worked for a long time. In fact for the longest time after that I believed that a boycott was the best way to go. I felt that we should have disengaged completely, and not given them legitimacy by seeming to engage in the process. .

But in that meeting with Basoga Nsadhu, William Pike who was the Chief Editor of the government owned *New Vision* admitted that he supported Museveni and the Movement, but said that his partisan views did not interfere with the paper's neutral reporting. To imagine that the Chief Editor of a newspaper would sit in such a meeting and say that – it was so contradictory! How were we supposed to trust his editorial policy after that? But even worse – Basoga Nsadhu who was chairing the meeting came in straight from Eastern Uganda where he had been campaigning for Museveni, and he was wearing a Museveni campaign T-shirt. This was an official government meeting. He was not in this meeting as Museveni's agent, but as a government Minister. That was the big problem we had, of failure to separate the party from the state. At that time it was even more difficult, because the Movement had not declared itself as a party yet. We were all supposed to be under a single party system.[29]

A lively and constantly updated Web site, complete with a huge picture gallery of the campaign trail, enabled the Elect Kizza Besigye Task Force to interact with ardent supporters and fierce critics alike. The campaign had a dedicated photographer who covered the rallies. This enabled the campaign to upload the latest rally pictures onto the Web site with relative ease, courtesy of a small but efficient IT company in whose offices I sat to do the work. The company was hosting the RA Web site, and it turned out that they were also hosting the Museveni Web site. Although we wanted to believe that the proprietor, Edward Balidawa, was an RA supporter, it was hard to say for sure. He seemed quite happy to serve two masters. A few years later he did declare himself to be a Movement supporter, and he even successfully ran for Parliament on a Movement ticket. But media coverage was a constant struggle. Anne Mugisha described it to me thus:

---

29   Interview with Anne Mugisha, April 2009.

The 2001 campaign was characterized by media that was openly and blatantly anti-opposition. At that time the only TV that had the capacity to cover upcountry events was UTV. Not only did they refuse to give Reform Agenda [Elect Kizza Besigye Task Force] journalists to cover Reform Agenda events and rallies, but even when we funded the journalists to travel to these events, and got the footage and other materials, they were usually unwilling to put them on air. WBS was the only private television, and it was instrumental in exposing how far the state was willing to go to stifle opposition in the Rabwoni[30] saga. It was the only TV that covered that airport fiasco.

---

30   Retired Major Okwir Rabwoni was a former Member of Parliament, and a national youth coordinator for the Elect Kizza Besigye Task Force. His brother Noble Mayombo, Chief of Military Intelligence, was a vocal and influential Museveni supporter. Rabwoni was violently arrested during the campaign.

Chapter 6: Your Brother's Keeper, Your Brother's Captor

'Our mandate was a limited one: to fight to restore freedom, by which we meant that the people should be given the chance to decide on their own destiny, without manipulation.'[31] – Yoweri Museveni

On 20 February 2001, just three weeks to the presidential polls, Besigye set out to address a series of rallies in Arua, West Nile, in the company of Okwir Rabwoni, Head of the youth desk at the Elect Kizza Besigye Task Force. That Rabwoni was a key figure in the Besigye campaign was itself a source of keen interest; his brother Noble Mayombo was Head of the Chieftaincy of Military Intelligence (CMI) and a well-known and vocal supporter of Museveni.[32] Besigye and Rabwoni, with several other Reform Agenda leaders in the entourage, arrived at Entebbe airport prepared to take their flight to

31   Yoweri Kaguta Museveni, 'Fighting Obote', *Sowing the Mustard Seed* (London & Basingstoke: Macmillan Publishers Ltd, 1997).

32   Mayombo was an Army Representative in the Constituent Assembly that wrote the 1995 Uganda Constitution. Subsequently he served as Museveni's aide de camp (1996–1997) before moving to the Chieftaincy of Military Intelligence. Between 2000 and 2004, when he headed the CMI, many secret detention centres or 'safe houses' were created, where alleged rebels, 'terrorists', and opponents of the NRM regime were often kept incommunicado and tortured. Although the electoral laws prohibited the military from involvement in politics, Mayombo was accused of harassing Museveni's opponents, distributing money to fund Museveni's campaigns, and directly campaigning for him. In 2005, Mayombo was promoted to Brigadier and appointed Permanent Secretary at the Ministry of Defence, as well as Board Chair of the state-owned *New Vision* newspaper. He died on 1 May 2007 after a short illness, leaving behind a trail of rumours about what or who killed him.

Arua. That is as far as they went. The events that followed were for many people the first indication that the regime had taken leave of all pretences at civility in order to secure a Museveni victory at all costs.

'The first time I knew there was something afoot with Rabwoni,' recounted Anne Mugisha, 'was through a phone call from a young reporter at CBS [Central Broadcasting Service].'

> She said, 'We have heard that Rabwoni has crossed to the Movement. Would you please comment?' Rabwoni had spent a weekend in the company of Tinyefuza[33] in Ssembabule. To this day we do not know what transpired during that weekend. Before this he had been through all sorts of intimidation and he had stood his ground. He had been stripped of his firearms, he was constantly harassed, and he was being followed everywhere – I could not believe that he of all people would join the Movement. I called him right away, and he answered the phone. 'Anne, I cannot talk now, but there is something I am working on. Be patient, I will explain everything.' He was whispering into the phone.

---

33   David Tinyefuza is a lawyer and bush war veteran of the NRA. He was known for, among other things, his tough (and some say ruthless) leadership of Operation North, a military operation that was supposed to rid northern Uganda of Kony and his Lord's Resistance Army. In 1996, while still Major General, Tinyefuza tried to quit the army following a contentious testimony that he gave while appearing before the Parliamentary Committee on Defence and Internal Affairs. His resignation letter stated in part, 'I am of the strong view that I will not have that constitutional right [to be treated fairly and justly] before the UPDF High Command for obvious reasons. It is therefore, because of the above that I must resign from the Army and subsequently it's High Command. I find it un-justified to continue serving in an institution whose bodies I have no faith in or whose views I do not subscribe to.' His resignation was refused. He petitioned the Constitutional Court and won the case but lost when the government appealed in the Supreme Court. His resignation having failed, Tinyefuza remained in the UPDF. He subsequently got promoted to full General and has become fiercely loyal to Museveni.

'Rabwoni, I need to know now. I need to tell the press something. Have you crossed or not?'

'Be patient – I will explain.' And the line went dead.

Shortly after that Grace Kavuya, treasurer for the Elect Besigye Task Force, stormed into my apartment seething with anger. 'How could he do this to us?' she kept asking. The news was on the FM stations. We did not have to wonder for long. About half an hour later there was a knock on the door – and in walked Rabwoni with his beautiful wife Solange. Before Grace and I could get the questions out, he announced rather dramatically, 'I need a lift [ride] to the American Embassy. Now.' We tried to ask what the urgency was about but he would not tell us.

'If they catch me I will be finished. You do not know what these people are capable of.' The situation was even more confusing for us, because when we asked him where he had found the car that brought him to my house he said it belonged to Major General Tinyefuza – one of the people he was supposedly running away from. He was visibly terrified, and kept saying he had to get to the American Embassy before 'they' found him. As it happened the day was an American pubic holiday so the Embassy was closed. We decided to drive to the Ambassador's residence. The security officers at the gate whisked us off to another house, where Rabwoni was taken into the premises. Grace, Solange, and I waited outside. After about two hours Rabwoni emerged.

'The Embassy says they cannot help me as long as I am in the country. They have advised me to find some means to get out of the country.' So we drove away with our hot passengers. On our way back into town we needed to fuel the car and I realized that in the haste to get Rabwoni to the embassy I had left my purse at home. To our surprise he pulled out a hefty stack of brand new 20,000 shilling bills – clearly he was loaded. Grace and I were not sure if all this talk about his need to get out of the country was not a ruse. We called KB [Kizza Besigye] to ask for his advice. His instructions were clear and firm – to drive to his residence in Luzira and stay put until he got there. If we thought that Rabwoni's bag of tricks was exhausted, we were to be surprised even further. At Besigye's gate he pulled a pistol out of his pocket and surrendered it to the guard without waiting to be asked. Grace could have killed him with her bare hands.

'What? What are you doing with a gun at our candidate's house? Have you come to kill him?' She was livid.

'Did you know I had the gun? Have I not surrendered it voluntarily?' Rabwoni appeared pained by the suggestion that he could have been harbouring ill motives.

After we settled into the house I called Andrew Mwenda, an investigative journalist with the *Monitor*. I told him that I had heard some rumours making the rounds that Rabwoni had crossed to the movement, but that I had him by my side, and he was still on the Besigye team.

'Impossible!' he countered.

To save him asking too many questions I put Rabwoni on the line. They chatted away for a while, and we then agreed that Mwenda could come out and take some pictures for the *Monitor* when Besigye came home.[34]

The following day was a bonanza for the media. On the one hand the *New Vision* had a huge headline proclaiming that Rabwoni had crossed. On the other was the *Monitor*, with a front page picture of

34   Author's interview with Anne Mugisha, March 2009.

Rabwoni and Mwenda at Besigye's house, in the company of hosts Besigye and Winnie, clearly in a celebratory mood complete with champagne glasses in hand. And that is when Rabwoni's troubles started in earnest. It turned out that a few days before, Amelia Kyambadde, Museveni's principal private secretary, had organized a youth conference at Ranch on the Lake (a lakeside hotel), at which Rabwoni was to speak regarding his decision to abandon the opposition. He was a no-show. It was said that he had been paid handsomely for his coming to speak at the conference. Now he had spent the evening dining and wining with the same opposition he was supposed to have ditched. If this were true, then it was no wonder that he wanted a quick exit from the country. He was going to pay – and it would not be cheap.

While the press was having a ball over all these contradictions, reality started to hit home for Rabwoni. There were many people with egg on their faces as a result of his antics: Amelia Kyambadde, Rabwoni's brother Mayombo, and the *New Vision* with their lead story, to name a few. It was clear the Movement would come after him. There were suggestions from some people that he be taken out of the country to avoid nasty reprisals, but Besigye maintained that if he stayed with him, there was nothing the Movement could do to him. That is how Rabwoni ended up on the Arua-bound delegation in Entebbe.

As Publicity Secretary for the Besigye Task Force, Anne Mugisha followed the developments closely:

> Someone called and told me there was some serious confusion at the airport that it involved the military, and that Besigye and Rabwoni were at the centre of it. I immediately called Andrew Mwenda.
>
> 'Mwenda – there is some major chaos at the airport; it seems there might be some shooting as well. You may want to get there fast!' He must have grown wings.
>
> It emerged that Moses Rwakitarate[35] was in charge of

35   Captain Moses Rwakitarate was the Intelligence Officer in State House. He was later promoted to Colonel and appointed Chief of Staff of the UPDF Air Force.

the military forces, and that the state was going to do all in their powers to stop Rabwoni from going with Besigye. Very rapidly the situation degenerated into a tussle, with Besigye literally hanging onto Rabwoni's rather spare frame to prevent the soldiers from taking him away. The ladies in the group were throwing their shoes and heckling the men. In the midst of all that the press arrived to witness this incredible spectacle being played out in the airport VIP lounge. The soldiers formed a ring around Besigye and Rabwoni, and moved in for the final grab. They threw Besigye into a chair and one of the soldiers knelt on his chest to keep him out of the action, as the others dragged Rabwoni away. As if on cue, at that very moment the East African Community Chairperson Dr. Muthaura and the Norwegian Ambassador matched into the lounge. 'Gentlemen, come and see how we are consolidating our democracy!' Besigye managed to say, breathless from the scuffle.

We later learnt that Rabwoni was thoroughly beaten, thrown aboard a pick-up truck, and taken to the CMI headquarters where he was held incommunicado for two days and without charge. So – that is the environment in which we naively thought we could win an election and take over government.[36]

Mugisha became animated as she recounted the story. A lawyer by training, she had spent a decade pleading the case for social justice and good governance in Uganda without stepping in a courtroom once. Her eyes either danced and twinkled or blazed – there seemed to be little in between. When she laughed she drew me into her laughter. Where did her immense energy come from? She seemed to have two sets of arms – one on her cell phone and one for her keyboard, which got no rest from the time she came home from work till she went to

---

36   Interview with Anne Mugisha, April 2009. I made repeated attempts to talk to Rabwoni while writing this story. He did not answer his phone and did not return my phone calls despite leaving detailed messages with his wife.

bed several hours later. She leafed through a book here, drank from a water bottle there, and patted her daughter's shoulder – all this while she talked. She pulled up documents, pictures, e-mails; between her computer and her head there was a huge resource for several volumes on Uganda's recent political history. I got the impression that she would be lost without her computer, which stayed online around the clock, with several windows open and running in the background. She might be living in Florida, but the inside of her home seemed to be located somewhere in Ugandan cyberspace.

Chapter 7: The Referee Is a Player on One of the Teams

'Not to be trusted is the greatest strategic handicap for any political group.' – Yoweri Museveni[37]

At the heart of all the 2000 and 2001 electioneering frenzy sat the Electoral Commission (EC). It was a body faced with numerous challenges, some of which it had brought upon itself. The Secretary to the Commission, its topmost officer, was recruited irregularly. Not only did Sam Rwakoojo lack the necessary experience according to the written opinion and advice of the Public Service Commission, but he was a business representative of Lithotec, a South African company doing business with the Electoral Commission. This clear conflict of interest did not deter his recruitment, which was made even more suspect because the position was not advertised as required. In 2002 when the Select [Parliamentary] Committee investigating electoral violence visited the EC, it discovered that eleven of the twenty-one senior employees were not qualified to hold the jobs that they did. Most had been hired irregularly; they had been seconded by 'big people'. Data processing, finance, civic education, and human resources were all in unqualified hands. It would seem that the Commission, having been either unable or unwilling to exercise independence in these crucial recruitment decisions, was later unable to resist further external interferences once the personnel were on board.

Investigations into the workings of the EC revealed problems with all phases of the electoral process – from equipping it to voter

37   Yoweri Kaguta Museveni, 'Fighting Obote', *Sowing the Mustard Seed* (London & Basingstoke: Macmillan Publishers Ltd, 1997).

registration, civic education, supervision of the polls, the tallying process, and financial impropriety.[38] There were instances where civic educators, paid by the EC to sensitise the voters, also doubled as campaign agents for the Movement candidates.

The running of the Electoral Commission was a study in mismanagement. In June 1999 the Commission purchased a printing press from a foreign company. At 700 million Uganda shillings (US$465,000), this was probably an excellent investment. Large quantities of printed materials were going to be needed in the run-up to the elections. The machine was delivered in December of the same year. In the six months following the delivery of the printing press, the EC spent more than half the cost of the machine in printing expenses – not using the printing press, but paying outside commercial printers. The machine was still nicely wrapped in its original packaging, lying in the Commission's backyard; it had never been entered into the EC inventory books. It was not installed until several months later, after the Auditor General pointed out what savings could have been made with the use of the machine.

In 2000 the Electoral Commission started making double payments to some districts for referendum-related expenses. They concealed the payments by providing false accountability. One revealing example included receipts and invoices from the Mubende district for vehicles whose registration numbers had not even been issued by the Ministry of Works. An employee of the district confessed that the money was shared with the officers of the Commission.

Many other strange things happened at the Electoral Commission, then headed by Hajji Aziz Kasujja. The EC was operating several accounts with commercial banks and moving large sums of money from their statutory accounts in Bank of Uganda into these accounts with little accountability – and without the knowledge of the Commissioner in charge of overseeing finance. The EC deposited some of the money with Prime Forex Bureau Limited, a financial institution not permitted by law to take deposits from its clients. Out of this irregular deposit, money was withdrawn in foreign and local currency in cash.

38   'Report for the Parliamentary Committee on Election Violence', July 2002.

It was discovered that Mr. Kasujja and his Commissioners were paying themselves monthly gratuity through M/s Millennium, a UK–based company.

Procurement at the EC seemed to consist of a painstaking process of separating the rational from the irrational, the clean from the dubious, the straightforward from the convoluted – and having thus set the two piles apart, the procurement process was completed by throwing out everything rational and above board. A case in point: In March 2001 the EC ordered for special materials from M/S Omicron Corporation Inc. in the United States to make photo identity cards. They paid for the materials, freight, and insurance. The consignment was expected to take three to four weeks for delivery at Entebbe. Then for some inexplicable reason, the EC turned around and chartered a plane to fly the materials to Entebbe at an extra cost of US$220,000. The hot goods were then put away for months and were in fact not used for their intended purpose.

The Chairman and three of the Commissioners had shares in, or fully owned, companies that were doing business with the EC. While they did not deny this, they claimed that they never influenced the EC to give business to these companies.

The EC leaked detailed information about upcoming bids for ballot papers and related materials to their preferred company, Lithotec, whose representative was being hired as the Secretary to the Commission. When the EC was told by Central Tender Board that they had to use competitive bidding, they faxed information to three other companies. The faxes were sent on Friday evening, and the companies were told the deadline for submission of the proposals was Tuesday morning with no possible extension. Lithotec had been given the information months previously. It was no surprise therefore that the company got the contract to print the ballot papers. After delivery it was discovered that there were serious 'mix-ups' with the ballots. Lithotec told the EC not to worry; they would quickly correct their own mistakes at extra cost to the EC. The company determined their own terms and prices, and the Electoral Commission was so trusting that they did not think it necessary to investigate the cause of the said mix-ups, so the EC forked out a further US$297,000 to fix something whose exact nature they did not quite comprehend.[39]

The EC purchased 5,000 computer disks to be used in the voter registration exercise. Out of the 5,000 disks purchased, 1,000 were issued to the relevant department, and only 12 were ever used. The whole super-disk venture was ill conceived, and in any case the disks were supplied when the voter registration had already ended.

But the undisputed prize in this orgy of mismanagement goes to the EC's bungled attempts to produce photographic voter identification (PVI) cards and put in place a voters' register. The EC could not have done worse if it had invited a friendly country to come and run it for them. As it is, they had teams of commissioners and senior management staff touring a number of countries in Europe, North America, and South Africa, ostensibly to shop for the right system. It was the equivalent of sending people to go and purchase various car parts from different car manufacturers, and then hiring a consultant mechanic to put together a car – in the case of the EC, with a tight deadline of twenty-one days. The incompatibility problems that emerged in the voter registration system had been anticipated by SWIPCO, a Swiss procurement company contracted by the Ugandan government to provide procurement audit services. SWIPCO advised against the venture. In May 2002, the project was determined to have cost almost US$4,369,000 over the envisaged total cost of US$7,767,200, and it was nowhere near finished. To crown it all, the Minister of Finance said that the whole project had not been budgeted for and that the EC had unilaterally diverted the funds from other planned activities. The Inspector General of Government (IGG) noted that the entire project execution and management had been characterised by 'crisis management and lack of forward planning, both of which gave golden opportunities for corruption, and embezzlement of public funds leading to massive financial losses to the Ugandan tax payers'.

Citing these and many other examples, including the loss of more than 2 billion shillings [US$1.3 million] of public funds through

39   Inspectorate of Government Report, *A Report of the Inspectorate on Favouritism in the Award of the Tender to Lithotec to Supply Ballot Papers to the EC*, May 2002.

open violation of regulations, the Inspector General of Government declared the EC incompetent and lacking integrity.[40] The IGG's final conclusion? 'By way of conclusion, it would be appropriate to state that anything that could be done to mismanage an organisation has been done in the EC.' This statement would have been a source of hilarious laughter had it been in reference to the management of a roadside kiosk, or the referee of a village football match. But this was the national EC, headed by men and women that were handpicked and endorsed by the President, and entrusted with the management of all elections in the country. This was the team that the Attorney General would be called upon time and again to defend with a straight face.

The presidential election took place on 12 March 2001. The country held its breath. An initial lead by the opposition was soon overturned when the results from the rural areas started to come in. At that point most Ugandans were still unaware of the hundreds of polling stations that had been created just days before the polls – some of them made known to the opposition candidates on the eve of the poll. Neither was the unmonitored voting within military barracks common knowledge, or the numerous other ways in which the state machinery had been deployed to ensure the victory of the incumbent, such as forcing voters to tick the ballot papers in front of the state agents, and chasing agents of the opposition from polling stations. Anne Mugisha described the mood on the night the results were announced:

> We had started off not quite understanding, or wanting to believe the extent to which Museveni would go to retain power. There was some illusion. There were comments from our leaders that I would recall much later and realize that they had seriously misjudged Museveni's capacity for deception. I think the moment of truth though, was the night of the results. We knew the whole country was waiting to hear the results. KB [Kizza Besigye], Winnie

40   *Report of the Select Committee on Election Violence and Other Related Matters*, 2002.

Byanyima, Winnie Babihuga, and I were at KB's house in Luzira. When the results started to come in, there was an expression of complete bafflement on KB's face. None of us had been prepared for the magnitude of the electoral theft that had just occurred. What we had not grasped, from the campaign agents in the villages, probably right through to the top leadership; was that Museveni would not allow a fair race under any circumstances. It was not enough to have supporters. It was not enough for those supporters to vote for the opposition candidate. It was critical for the voters to stay by the ballot box and defend their votes with their very lives. At that time we could not imagine that the incumbent could engage in electoral theft on a grand scale – after all had he not waged a bloody war on the premise of a rigged election?

Anne said this while laughing at the sheer absurdity of this contradiction.

We did not know the tricks they were using to steal votes. We did not know of extra ballot papers, or overnight stuffing of ballot boxes. That is why it took people like Besigye so long to admit, even to themselves, that they were conned into supporting the bush war. It is not easy to admit that you were fooled – that you were gullible. That has been the response of other people who participated in the bush war. People like Mugisha Muntu and Amanya Mushega[41]; they all find it difficult to admit that they were used by a cunning and charismatic leader who lured them using platitudes that he never intended to follow. It takes a long time for anyone to admit that they were so wrong at such a fundamental level. At a grander scale we see the same denial in U.S. policy towards Uganda. It cannot change overnight. Do not

---

41   In my conversations with Muntu, he readily acknowledged that Museveni had 'outwitted' them.

forget that it was an American president that came to Uganda and told the world that Ugandan leadership was a beacon of hope for the region. The U.S. does not want to rewrite its foreign policy manual on Uganda, and nobody wants to admit that they completely misjudged the quality of Uganda's leadership. It would only reflect poorly on U.S. policy advisors.[42]

The results were received with mixed emotions, and within hours of the announcements the Elect Kizza Besigye Task Force had announced its intention to contest the results through a court petition.

The parliamentary elections were just as violent and chaotic as the presidential elections, and in many places probably even more so. In Rukungiri, the outcome of the election of the Woman Member of Parliament was contested in court. At the conclusion of the petition hearing, the judges summarised the findings on the Electoral Commission thus:

> The evidence adduced proves deliberate use of one of the worst voters' registers that can be found anywhere during democratic elections. [The voters' register was hand written.]
>
> Use of election officers ... who sympathetically facilitated the strong-armed methods of intimidation of voters employed by government officers and members of security organs at many polling stations, or who manifestly participated in ticking ballot papers for voters or in forcing voters to tick ballot papers in the open at the presiding officer's table or in falsifying results of the poll.
>
> Use of an irretrievably defective register of voters, which led to widespread multiple registration and voting impersonation, and all forms of election abuse that a worthless voters' register is susceptible to.

---

42 Interview with Anne Mugisha, April 2009.

> Failure by the Electoral Commission to issue clear
> and comprehensive election guidelines to field
> election officers thus rendering the election more or
> less an in-house affair for the chiefs and LCs [Local
> Councils], thus exposing it to extensive abuse…

> Widespread intimidation of the electorate by the
> RDCs [Resident District Commissioners] and
> security personnel in favour on one of the candidates
> before and during the voting process.[43]

In a contest between Amama Mbabazi[44] and opposition candidate
James Musinguzi Garuga, the judgment of the ensuing election
petition read like Murphy's law – anything that could go wrong did
go wrong. The Resident District Commissioner and serving military
officers traversed the constituency campaigning for Mbabazi. In
one incident soldiers of the Presidential Protection Unit under the
command of Captain Ndahura intercepted and violently dispersed
Musinguzi's procession of supporters following a rally in Kihihi
town. On the same day, one of Musinguzi's campaign vehicles
was intercepted by soldiers, among them Capt. Ndahura's escort.
The vehicle occupants were physically assaulted; a public address
system mounted on the vehicle was taken away, as was all the money
they had. The soldiers wantonly smashed the windscreen for good
measure.

---

43   Judgment of the High Court of Uganda at Mbarara (Mr. Justice Kibu-
uka-Musoke) Electoral Petition No. 4 of 2001, Babihuga versus Masiko Komuhangi; Judgment of the Court of Appeal of Uganda in Kampala, Election petition
No. 9 of 2002, Masiko Komuhangi versus Babihuga.

44   Amama Mbabazi is Minister of Security. He previously held the port-
folios of Minister of State in the President's office, Minister of State for Defence
(1986–1992), Minister of State for Foreign Affairs, Attorney General, and Minister of Defence. In late 2008, Mbabazi became embroiled in a battle with Parliament over the 'Temangalo' scandal, in which he allegedly pressured the National
Social Security Fund (agency responsible for the collection, safekeeping, invest-
ment, and distribution of workers' retirement funds) to buy a piece of his land for
over US$6 million. A parliamentary probe committee was appointed to investi-
gate the scandal. During the probe the Managing Director of the Fund claimed
that he was pressured to pay the money. President Museveni spoke in Mbabazi's
defence, and the inquiry appears to have ceased.

A week later, one of Mbabazi's campaign agents who was also an employee of the paramilitary Internal Security Organisation (ISO) trailed and shot at a vehicle carrying Twinomuhwezi, Musinguzi's campaign mobiliser. The vehicle occupants were injured. One of the men was injured in the face, resulting in loss of the eye. (The man who fired at the car was bearing the firearm illegally and was by law prohibited from serving as a campaign agent because he was employed by the ISO. During the election petition hearing, Mbabazi's defence wanted this part of the evidence excluded because they said the mobiliser lied when he implied that the eye was injured by the bullet. They claimed that the injury was a result of broken glass from the shattered windscreen.) The petition was successful, and the court overturned the election and declared the seat vacant. Mbabazi appealed the court ruling and lost.

The appeals court judge noted, 'The campaigns in this constituency had been characterized by violence and intimidation which persisted unabated up to the voting day. Several polling stations were invaded by soldiers in company of the 1st appellant's [Amama Mbabazi] agents. They assaulted and arrested the respondent's [Musinguzi] agents and mounted road blocks on the way to many polling centres. All these instilled fear in the minds of the voters and paved the way for voting malpractices. These proved failures to comply with the provisions of and principles laid down in the Act. That there was non-compliance with the provisions of and principles of the Act [Parliamentary Elections Act] was in fact not seriously disputed.'

Despite the two court rulings against Mbabazi, he was still eligible to run in the by-election because the law did not bar persons found guilty of electoral crimes from participating in subsequent elections. As Minister of Defence, Mbabazi was allowed to keep all his military detail around him in the campaign for the by-election. It was reported that more than 7,000 soldiers were deployed in the constituency. Fearing the worst for himself and his supporters, Musinguzi abandoned the contest, and Mbabazi was announced the default winner. The bulk of the offences committed during the campaigns were neither investigated nor prosecuted.

Another election that attracted great attention was that of Winnie

Byanyima, Dr. Kizza Besigye's wife. Journalist Charles Onyango Obbo described Byanyima's return to Parliament after a bitter contest between her and Movement candidate Ngoma Ngime as 'possibly the most massive failed effort anywhere in the world to unseat an incumbent MP'. In the weeks leading to the poll, Mbarara was swarmed by the army (mainly the PPU) and State House staff and security operatives to alternately harass and bribe voters to abandon Byanyima. Not relying on these tactics alone to deliver the election, the state also engaged in vote rigging. In one incident Ngoma Ngime's driver and body guard, Amanya, shot Johnson Tumusiime, a Byanyima supporter. Both of Tumusiime's legs were shattered, though he survived. (When the Select Parliamentary Committee of Electoral Violence visited Mbarara a year after the elections, Tumusiime was still not able to work. In the meantime Amanya had not been prosecuted but was reported to have been promoted and transferred.) The tension was almost unbearable when the vote counting got underway. It was clearly not a contest between Byanyima and Ngime; it was between the Besigye/Byanyima duo and Museveni. I was in the hospital that day, and someone brought a radio to the casualty department. When the news broke that Byanyima had won – after an initial scare that showed Ngime in the lead – the wild cheering that broke out was a sign of how much emotion people had invested in this one election.

The end of the 2001 presidential and parliamentary campaigns did not bring relief to the vanquished opposition. There were frequent reports of intimidation and torture of those who had supported the opposition by agents linked to the state. Many people who had participated actively in the campaigns went back to their jobs. It did not take long for the reprisals to begin. Some people lost their jobs, and the government sent the message that to support an opposition candidate was to bite the hand that feeds you. Conrad Nkutu was an early victim; he was fired from his job as company secretary of the government-owned *New Vision* newspaper. Opposition politicians who had business loans were easy targets – suddenly the loans would be called, and if they were not fully paid up, the businesses were shut down or sold. It soon became the pattern that to get government employment or contracts, one had to declare their political affiliation. (By 2006 this practice had become so entrenched that Moses Kigongo, the Chairman of the Movement Party, told a rally in Ntungamo on 12 January 2006 that 'only supporters of the Movement will get jobs after the election'.[45])

On 19 August 2001, local newspapers carried startling news. Splashed across the front pages of both major dailies were screaming headlines reporting Besigye's disappearance. The days that followed were full of speculation. Rumours were rife. The cartoonists had a field day, depicting Besigye as having fled the country dressed in a *busuuti* (a lady's voluminous outfit worn mostly in central and eastern Uganda) complete with a head scarf. One account said that he had recorded himself talking and had escaped from under the noses of the state security guys by leaving the tape playing. From outside the house, the guards would have heard his voice clearly and would have had no reason to believe that he was not in the house. Apparently he was not missed until a whole night and part of the morning had gone by. Regarding his mode of escape and his whereabouts, I was just as ignorant as anybody else.

Besigye left the country after a series of security incidents that had become increasingly more sinister. He had been prevented from boarding planes, was constantly and overtly trailed by an assortment of security agents, and was on one occasion nearly abducted by men in UPDF[46] uniform on Masaka–Mbarara Road. The intimidation and harassment did not cease for the supporters he left behind, or for anyone who did not support the Movement.

In the months following Besigye's departure, many other people crossed the border into exile. I have met mostly young men in Kenya and South Africa who were hounded out of their homes for having been Besigye campaigners and polling agents. One man fled Kamwenge in Western Uganda after his house was torched on the eve of the presidential poll. The exiles were often described as self-imposed. I often wondered which other types there were. Was there, for instance, a state-sponsored, 'all expenses paid' exile?

45   'Has Kigongo joined the victimization advocates?' *Monitor*, 18 January 2006.
46   The National Resistance Army (NRA) was renamed the Uganda People's Defence Forces (UPDF)

Chapter 8: We Have Culprits, Now Let's Find the Crime

'Let me take this opportunity to reiterate what I have said many times before, that the NRM government is fully committed to the rule of law, the protection of individual human rights, and the independence of the judiciary. Our country has gone through a traumatic experience for the last twenty or so years, mainly because Obote and Amin had no respect for the rule of law. Their soldiers and security agents had become a law unto themselves because they could murder, rape, and rob with impunity. The liberation war was fought to restore the dignity and inviolability of the person of every Ugandan and to protect his property. Nobody has the right to take away a person's life, freedom, or property except within the due process of the law.' – Yoweri Museveni [47]

On 12 February 2002, in the run-up to the local council elections, Alfred Bongomin, the Movement Chairperson for Pabbo sub-county in Gulu district, was murdered by unknown persons. This led to a cascade of arrests of opposition politicians. One week after the murder, Steven Olanya and Peter Oloya Yumbe were arrested as suspects. These two were actively campaigning for Kerubino Uma, an opposition politician running against Lt. Col. Walter Ochola. Yumbe had also been a very active campaigner of other opposition politicians, including Nobert Mao and Betty Aol. Several other opposition activists, including David Penytoo (later to become a Member of Parliament) and Tony Kitara, were also arrested and

---

47   Yoweri K. Museveni, 'Colonial versus Modern Law', a speech at a law seminar in Kampala, 12 January 1987, in *What Is Africa's problem?* (Minnesota University Press, 2000).

charged with treason. On the night of 16 September 2002, soldiers from the UPDF raided Gulu Central Prison in an apparent move to forcefully take the suspects to the military barracks. In the scuffle Peter Oloya Yumbe was gunned down and killed in the prison compound. Betty Aol, a Member of Parliament for Gulu, had known Yumbe very well, and on hearing that he had died she went to his home to console the family. She told me about Yumbe's death.

> He [Yumbe] was a tall and fearless man. If there was any intimidation, Yumbe would be there. If one [of us] was in trouble, you could see how Yumbe would run. He had campaigned actively for [Norbert] Mao and for me as well in the 2001 elections. The Movement wanted to get him on their side, and they failed. They tried to implicate him in something but there was nothing. When Alpeo [Alfred Bongomin] was killed, they found a way of implicating Yumbe. But luckily for him, some people in the Movement went and stood witness for him in court – that at the time of the murder Yumbe was with these men in a bar drinking, twenty-five kilometres from where the man was killed. So he was cleared, but he was still sent back to prison. The night he was killed, a military intelligence officer went to the prison on the pretext that he wanted to relocate the prisoners. He ordered the shooting of Yumbe. This man [Yumbe] was in Gulu central prison, he was surrounded by security, and he was unarmed. Why would anybody shoot and kill such a man?

After a short pause, during which I could not find anything appropriate to say, Aol went on.

> So the next morning we got to know that Yumbe had been killed. We went to his home. He [had been] taking care of his brother's orphans. He also had his own children. They were all there. The mother was there. She was already preparing to bury her son. 'Lokang, lokang' she kept saying. In Acholi this

means 'firstborn'. It seems Yumbe was her firstborn, so she kept repeating over and over again: 'Lokang, lokang.' We started preparing for the burial, but the body was not released. We waited; days turned into weeks, then into months, and now years. Up to today the body has never been released. The family never got an opportunity to bury their son and father. The intelligence officer was promoted. The police tried, and human rights organizations tried, to get the body released, but they all failed. Now some people are saying, 'Oh, don't talk about it. Let the family be given compensation.' [But] the children are there. They will grow up, and one day they will ask.[48]

There was no investigation into Yumbe's death. The Intelligence Officer who organised the shooting got a promotion about a year after the prison incident. Some of the men who had been arrested at the same time as Yumbe were later persuaded by government agents to apply for amnesty in order to gain their freedom. In 2003 the state withdrew the murder charge against Olanya, and he was freed. Penytoo was also released at about the same time.

Following their release, the two politicians immediately resumed political activity and were, on at least two occasions, confronted by security agencies over holding FDC meetings.

On 9 March 2005 Olanya and Penytoo were picked up by the police over an allegation that they were involved in some shootings. In a strange twist, just as the police were letting them go for lack of evidence, they were arrested by the UPDF and taken to the army barracks. The following day they were joined by another activist, Ochan Laryang. The three men reported that during their detention they were repeatedly told that if they did not abandon their political activities and declare support for the Movement, they would remain in custody – or worse. On 25 March the prisoners were moved from

48   Interview with Honourable Betty Aol, Woman Member of Parliament for Gulu, February 2010. In 2009 while on a trip to Gulu, Museveni was asked about Yumbe's body. He expressed surprise, and instructed that the body should be released to the relatives. This has still not happened.

Gulu barracks and taken to the Central Police Station in Kampala. To their shock and horror, they were then told to make statements concerning their role in the murder of the late Resident District Commissioner for Kitgum, Ochaya, which the police said had happened in 2002. (Actually, Ochaya had died in 1999.) Despite the glaring contradictions, the three men remained in detention until 5 April, when their lawyer secured an order for their release. At that point the police said the prisoners were the business of the UPDF and that only the army could release them. The following day, almost a month after they had been arrested by the military, Olanya, Penytoo, and Ochan Laryang were produced in court and this time charged with the murder of Alfred Bongomin!

Following this bizarre turn of events, the Members of Parliament from Gulu met with several top government officials to explain to them that the murder charges were politically motivated and intended to keep the activists out of circulation. A couple of weeks later, their appeals got a dramatic response. On 20 April 2005, two of these politicians, Reagan Okumu and Michael Ocula, were also arrested and charged with the murder of the same Alfred Bongomin. At that point it would have been difficult for them to take comfort in Museveni's assurances regarding the necessity of the due process of the law.

The death of Alfred Bongomin was a brutal crime. His life was taken away in a most violent manner, probably for attempting to participate in a legitimate electoral process, in a country not at war. The least the law enforcers could do was bring the perpetrators of this crime to justice. There was no evidence that this was being done. Investigations into the murder of Peter Oloya Yumbe should have been easier because it occurred in the prison compound, in full view of several persons, and in the presence of easily identifiable armed persons. His extrajudicial killing did not help the cause of justice.

Listening to Yumbe's story took me back several years. Between 1999 and early 2003, I made several trips to Gulu. The Injury Control Centre – Uganda, an organization that I headed at the time, had received a grant directed at reducing the effects of landmines in the war-ravaged north. I and Ronald Lett, a Canadian surgeon, led teams of doctors and other health workers to train various groups in emergency trauma care, in partnership with a friend and colleague, Martin Ogwang. Most of the people we trained were health workers, although on one occasion we trained members of the Gulu police and the UPDF's Fourth Battalion, the latter led by Dr. Musinguzi, an army doctor. The idea was to ensure that these armed forces personnel stationed in a volatile region would be able to efficiently evacuate injured people and provide them with appropriate first aid before transfer to the hospital. That was a fairly narrow agenda, and we stuck close to our mission. Later we received another grant that enabled us to expand our work to include the prevention of violence amongst young people. My visits to Gulu over that period were memorable for many reasons, and they influenced the manner in which I perceived interactions between government, the people of northern Uganda, and the rest of the country.

The Acholi region in which Gulu town is located is well acquainted with war and suffering. The colonial British administration recruited more heavily from this region proportionately than from other parts of the country to form the army. The composition of the army at independence was therefore ethnically imbalanced. When Idi Amin overthrew Obote in 1971, he purged the army, especially its top leadership, of Acholi soldiers. The return of Obote eight years later improved the fortunes of those that remained, but a good part of Obote's second presidency was spent at war – trying to route out various fighting groups, including the NRA. This put the Acholi at the head of the ensuing brutal armed conflict that resulted in heavy human and property losses especially in Buganda. Human rights abuses and looting of civilian property was commonplace. Because the Acholi constituted a large portion – up to 30% - of the government forces, many Ugandans still feel that they, or even more generally the 'northerners', were responsible for the war atrocities.

When the NRA took over power in 1986 the majority of the Acholi in the army fled to southern Sudan fearing deadly reprisals, but also seemingly to regroup and plan armed struggle. There has been armed conflict featuring different groups in northern Uganda since 1986, the most enduring being that led by Joseph Kony. Some see the various phases of the northern insurgency as a continuation of the Luwero conflict, with the war arena having shifted from the south to the north. There are questions concerning the failure of the NRA/UPDF to end the war in northern Uganda for more than two decades, even as the army expanded and sent troops on international peace keeping missions in places like Somalia. A whole generation has passed since the beginning of the Kony war, which has caused untold suffering among the people of Acholi – Kony's own people.

Ogwang was a surgeon at Lacor, an incredibly efficient mission hospital that treated the majority of the war injuries in the district. It was always refreshing to work with him and his team, including Richard, a young and very dedicated anaesthetist. We often started the day early and did not leave the hospital until after six in the evening. Except on one occasion when it was considered too insecure for me to commute between Lacor and Gulu, I usually stayed at a guest house in town. We would emerge from the hospital building at dusk to find the hospital compound rapidly turning into a refugee camp. There would be family groupings everywhere – under trees, along the veranda, and hurdled along the fence. The drive from the Lacor hospital gate to the town was the most revealing. Children ranging from as young as five to the early teens lined the entire stretch of that dusty road, some walking briskly, some half running, but a good number barely keeping up. This was the stream of night commuters going to spend the night in the relative safety of Gulu, to escape possible abduction by the Kony rebels in the villages. The children would sleep on the shop verandas or wherever they could find some form of shelter.[49] It was easier to see the children as a moving mass, but it was unbearable to look into the eyes of an individual child and to imagine what the mother must feel, letting her six-year-old girl undertake this trip night after night, never knowing if the child would return unharmed the following morning. Although the trauma care work usually went well and left us with a sense of accomplishment, I always returned to Kampala angry. Most Ugandans who had never been to northern Uganda treated Gulu as

49   Night commuting evolved into a complex phenomenon that eventually seemed to address other social needs beyond security from abduction. It also became more organized, with NGOs setting up centres for the commuters, where food and other services were provided. The numbers went down as relative peace returned to the region.

though it was part of another country. I would return with pictures of the children trudging along the dusty road at dusk still in my eyes. Life in Kampala appeared little affected by the war. Discussions about the northern Uganda war tended to be extremely polarized. On one hand there were those who were incoherent with frustration at how misunderstood the whole issue was. On the other hand were those to whom the war was some kind of academic puzzle to be debated and analysed but not necessarily ended. I also got to work with another doctor from northern Uganda, Chris Orach. Unlike Ogwang, who treated injured people one limb at a time, Orach worked in public health and had specialised in refugee health. Orach and Ogwang would have understood infinitely more about what was happening in Gulu because they spoke the language and understood the culture and history much better than I did.

I recall two incidents that happened just before these projects were completed. One morning I went to visit the Gulu Support the Children Organisation (GUSCO), an indigenous NGO working to promote the well-being of war-affected children in northern Uganda. GUSCO sometimes received children who had escaped from rebel captivity. That morning I found three boys who had arrived the previous evening. They had walked through the bush for eleven days after escaping from a rebel camp. Their feet and legs were swollen and sore, their bodies were emaciated, and their skins were scaly and scratched from their trek in the wild. I could not trust myself to speak when I was told that five boys had escaped, but that these three had watched as two of their colleagues died – or were too ill to move any further – somewhere along the way. It was inconceivable for me that eleven-year-old children were witnessing their friends die in the bush in the same country where their age mates were playing soccer in the Kampala Kids League on neatly manicured pitches.

The second incident arose from the violence prevention research that we conducted in primary schools in Gulu district. We wanted to know what type of conflicts children faced and how they resolved them. We wished to understand how they spent their time outside the classroom. Some children recounted how they would leave school in the evenings, go home only long enough to eat, and then, having changed from their school uniforms, go to the bush to hide for the night. It was known that the rebels would raid homesteads in the night to abduct children, so the parents would send the children off into the thickets where they must lie motionless and quiet to avoid detection. And here we were, coming from Kampala where children slept between bed sheets and under mosquito nets, and where a National Examinations Board regularly set exams to be sat by both sets of children – the ones from the thickets competing for the same opportunities as those from under bed nets. I did not know how long it would be before I returned to Gulu. Talking to Betty Aol nearly a decade later, I realised that a good proportion of those children I used to see on the Lacor road were now old enough to vote. It was disturbing to think about the kind of experiences that shaped their world view and influenced their choices.

Okumu and Ocula went to trial and were acquitted on 9 January 2006. Delivering the judgment, the High Court judge, Justice John Bosco Katutsi, said, 'A close study of the evidence tendered by prosecution shows clearly that it is a crude and amateur attempt at creative work.' Put plainly, the two politicians had been framed, but the state did not do a good job of it.

Chapter 9: No Safety in a Safe House

'The security of the people of Uganda is their right and not a favour bestowed by any regime. No regime has the right to kill any citizen of this country, or to beat any citizen at a roadblock. We make it clear to our soldiers that if they abuse any citizen, the punishment they will receive will teach them a lesson. As for killing people – if you kill a citizen, you yourself will be killed.' – Yoweri Museveni[50]

If anybody had told Ugandans in 1986 that the government planned to introduce secret houses where crime suspects would be held and tortured to extract confessions, and that these houses would be managed by persons not regularly employed or supervised by the prisons department, many would have been outraged. They would have questioned the legality of such actions. Some would not have believed that this could happen under the NRM government. In trying to understand how we got to the point where the existence of 'safe houses' is an open secret that does not provoke demonstrations, I asked John Nagenda, the Presidential Advisor on Media Affairs, about his views on this. I especially wanted to know whether he thought that the government had lost credibility and the moral authority to condemn previous governments, which were notorious for the running of torture houses. His response was unequivocal:

> It is a fact that however well-intentioned you are, to run a country you are going to have 'safe houses'. You are going to have so many things that happen. Maybe you do not experience them, maybe I hardly… notice

---

50   Yoweri Museveni, 'Ours Is a Fundamental Change', *What Is Africa's Problem?* (University of Minnesota Press, 2000).

them, but some people have to do the dirty work to keep you safe. I have never been against safe houses.

Any country in the world has safe houses. Any country in the world that feels really attacked will retaliate. I spent 1965 in the USA, and I wrote about this. There were some people at Kent University who were suspected by the government of being extremists. The government forces moved in and shot these people dead one night. In themselves these people were probably not very important. But the government wanted to send a message to extremists, to say, if you cause trouble, we shall kill you. Somebody noticed that all those people were shot at bed level – they had been sleeping. This was 1965. The American government did it. So – there are safe houses in London... there are safe houses in every country in the world.[51]

It is quite possible that some Ugandans believe, like Nagenda, that 'safe houses' and illegal detention are a necessary evil. What makes Nagenda's views particularly surprising is that he served as a Commissioner on the Commission of Inquiry into Violations of Human Rights that was set up by Museveni's Justice Ministry in May 1986. Chaired by Hon. Justice Arthur Oder, the Commission was mandated with investigating 'all aspects of human rights abuses' committed under previous governments from independence in 1962 until Museveni came into power on 25 January 1986. Commissioners were instructed to pay specific attention to arbitrary arrests, detentions, and killings. One of the Commission's key recommendations, contained in the 1994 report, was the repealing of laws that allowed for detention without trial. So what had happened to cause Nagenda such a serious change of heart?

In early 2009 I was introduced to a woman who said she had spent the better part of a year in a safe house. She looked and talked like the average woman in small-town Uganda. She and her husband owned a small general merchandise shop. She told me she used to

51   Interview with John Nagenda, May 2010.

72

trade in alcohol and owned a bar before her stay at the safe house. I was curious to know how she ended up in the safe house. For the next two hours, Kesanyu[52] ignored the shop and told me a story that kept me awake that night.

> Museveni persecutes people that vote against him. In the 2001 elections they said we could choose [the presidential candidate] who we wanted. I campaigned and voted for Besigye. What was wrong with that? My troubles started when I and my husband had gone to Kamwezi to trade in *waragi* [locally brewed gin]. On our way back we were arrested. We were seriously beaten even before we were taken to the police. It is the CMI [Chieftaincy of Military Intelligence; she pronounced it as *Si-Mwai*] and Local Defence Unit who beat us. When they eventually took us to the police, we had been so badly beaten, even they wondered what offence we could have committed. The CMI said we had been arrested having sex in a car. [Kesanyu laughed self-consciously.] Imagine – why would my husband and I leave our home to go and engage in such foolishness in Kamwezi? The following morning we were told we had been arrested for subversion against the government (*obuheekyera*).

> We were then transferred to Kabale Police Station. We were not charged with any offence; the police were told that we were there 'for safe custody'.

> We stayed there for fifteen days, during which time our relatives put a lot of pressure on the police to either charge us with some offence or let us go. In the end they decided to take us to the Mbarara military barracks. We were transferred under heavy military escort from Kabale and taken to the DISO [District Internal Security Officer], who was asked if he knew anything about me. He said his office had been watching me for several months and

52   Not real name. This woman requested that I do not disclose her identity.

monitoring my every move but had never seen me do anything suspicious. CMI had alleged that I was caught conferring with forty other people who were involved in subversion – they said the rest ran away.

Due to the intervention of many people, we were taken to the Mbarara police cells instead of the military barracks. We stayed there for three weeks. The government said they were undertaking investigations. I was very sick due to the beatings and torture that I had suffered. At that point I was passing pus from my private parts. Whenever I stood up, it [pus] would drain freely. I was very sick indeed, and the police were concerned that I might die in their custody. They insisted that either CMI take us to court or that they release us. Eventually we were released on police bond and told to report to Mbarara police every three days. Whenever we came to report, we were taken to the DISO's office, not the police station.

On one of those occasions when we had gone to report at DISO's office, we were kept waiting from around 9.00 AM until evening. At about 6.00 PM a gentleman came and told me to get into a waiting car and my husband to get into one of the offices. I thought we were going to be interrogated separately. The next thing I knew, the vehicle took off in the direction of Masaka. We did not stop anywhere until we were approaching Kampala. They did not tell me where I was being taken. When we got to the outskirts of Kampala, I was asked if I knew where we were. I said I thought it was Busega [a Kampala suburb]. They blindfolded me with an army jacket and kept on driving for another hour or so. I could tell that we were driving through heavy traffic. Then we parked somewhere, and the owner of the jacket they had used to blindfold me took it off and got out of the car. I looked around and saw that we were packed at CMI Headquarters on Kitante Road [Yusuf Lule Rd]. The men who remained in the car got another piece of cloth for the blindfold, and we drove off. I had no idea where we went, but when we finally stopped I was taken out of the car and told to start walking, still blindfolded. I was held by two people, one on either side. After a short distance I was told we were getting to a flight of steps, so I started climbing. Finally the blindfold was removed, and I was left in a dark corridor. In the morning I realized that I was not alone in the corridor. That is when it dawned on me that this must be one of the 'safe houses' I had heard about. There was a long table with cups of porridge, and I was given one of them. I figured that there were very many people – at least as many people as there were cups. I counted forty-six cups, and at lunch I was able to confirm this number from the plates. I stayed in that corridor for three days, and on the fourth day I was moved into a small room. Two nights later two Rwandese women were brought and put in the same room. They were taken away after three nights, and the rest of the time I spent in that house I was alone in the room. The windows had been painted black, so the only sense I had of daylight was a hazy lighting up around a tiny ventilator which was not well plugged. There was a light bulb, but its switch was in the guard room. The soldiers put it on when they came into the room, and they switched it off when they left. Usually they put on the light when the food was brought. Otherwise it was almost always dark. Then one night I was taken out to a car, blindfolded again, and driven to some location a fair distance from the house. When the vehicle stopped, I was taken out and marched into what seemed like a bush or a plantation, still blindfolded. When the blindfolding was eventually removed, I found us standing in front of what looked like graves. Everywhere it was dark except for the strong torches the men carried. They pointed to the long line of mounds of soil close together. Some of the mounds looked freshly dug, while others were overgrown with weeds and looked like they had been there for some time.

> 'Madam,' one of them started, 'if you do not tell us the truth about your activities, you will end up in one of these.'

> They started to shoot in the air. I was terrified. I knew my end had come.[53]

Kesanyu recounted how the soldiers argued among themselves concerning how to treat her, because they had so far failed to extract a confession. Some mentioned working on her fingers and nails, but in the end the man in charge decided against it, and they drove her back to the safe house. After that trip in the night, she was subjected

53   Interview with Kesanyu (not real name), May 2009.

to electrocutions. A metallic gadget would be handed to her, but as soon as she touched it she would be violently thrown against the wall. She described the pain of electrocution as being far worse than that of the beatings. All her clothes were taken away from her, and she was subjected to needle pricking of her nipples. She showed me her breasts, whose nipples were riddled with black scars, no longer their normal texture. She talked of being gang-raped by the soldiers several times. She recounted being chained to a metal rod and having to sleep in that position. As she spoke she uncovered her chest and arms to show me the scars. On several occasions the soldiers had asked her where her husband was, and she had told them that he was back at home. Then one night the soldiers brought her husband to her room.

> He looked awful. He was thin and looked older than I remembered him. I all along thought he had been released. My only comfort through all the suffering had been that he was out there doing all he could to find me. Now here he was. All hope left me. One of the soldiers was talking. He said that my husband had confessed and told them everything that I had been denying. At that point I really did not care – I had no idea what they might have forced him to confess. They left us in the room together, maybe to go and consult. For several moments we did not speak. Then my husband started talking. Even his voice sounded somewhat different.

> He narrated how he was captured. After I was driven away from Mbarara, he was allowed to go back home. The following day he went to Kampala and started appealing to all the people he thought could help to find me. There was no record of me in the police. He reported me as a missing person and narrated how I was driven away in a pick-up truck with government registration numbers. He went back home and was planning to report to the Mbarara police as usual. He was walking home from the bar one evening

when some unknown people grabbed him, gagged him, and bundled him into a car. He was driven to the DISO's house. He spent that night and all of the following day in the kitchen at the DISO's home. The following night a vehicle picked him up and brought him to the safe house.

Three days after husband and wife were reunited in the safe house, where they had both been living unknown to either of them, they were put in a pick-up truck and driven back to Mbarara. The man was taken to the Mbarara DISO's office and held there for two days. He was told that his wife, who was by now very ill and barely conscious, was being taken to the hospital. He was let go after it became public knowledge that the wife was undergoing treatment in Mbarara Hospital.

Kesanyu's admission to hospital seems to have happened more by good luck than by design. One evening in late 2004, some policemen were walking along the road outside Mbarara Hospital when one of them noticed a thin, unkempt woman lying in the trench. On closer observation by torchlight, they concluded that it was a mad woman who had probably been bumped off the road by a speeding car. Her hair was stringy and matted, clearly the result of no care for months. Her clothes looked unusually clean for one in such circumstances. They went over to the hospital, got a stretcher, and carried the woman into the hospital. The following morning one of the policemen dropped in at the hospital out of curiosity, to see if the woman had been identified and if she had survived. He found her still lying in the casualty department, her condition not much different from that of the previous night. The hospital staff thought she was homeless and merely in need of food. One of the nurses went over to the woman and uncovered her, planning to wipe her clean before they would examine her properly. She was startled to find the woman's entire backside covered with wounds that looked like the result of severe and repeated assaults – scars of all ages, infected wounds draining pus, as well as fresh-looking wounds from more recent assaults. She weighed only forty-one kilograms. It was clear this was no ordinary homeless woman. A female police officer was called in. The officer thought there was something vaguely familiar about the woman, and she remembered that several months back there had been a report of a missing woman. Her disappearance had been reported by, among others, a doctor who claimed to be related to her. Through some tenuous inquiries, the doctor was contacted and was able to establish that the moribund woman in Mbarara Hospital was his cousin, Kesanyu. Several weeks and many medical procedures later, Kesanyu was well enough to go home. She had been gone from her home for nine months altogether.

> A few days after I came home a man I did not know came to see me. He told me that they were aware I was contemplating taking my case to the Human Rights Court. [She called it 'woman right'.] He said the day I lodged a complaint concerning my ordeal I would be dead. I believed him.[54]

Where one might have expected that offenders should be arrested by the police except in extraneous situations, it had become common for the military or paramilitary personnel to arrest civilians and to detain them in the army barracks. At times the soldiers might arrest people and take them to the police for 'safe custody', or they might hold them in some ungazetted place. The demarcation of roles regarding the arrest and detention of civilians was very blurred, as Frank Atukunda, one of the men accused of belonging to a rebel group called the People's Redemption Army, was to discover.

> If I could have reached out to relieve the old man's suffering, I would have done so. He was probably in his late sixties. I momentarily forgot my own agony when I saw him swallow a few times, his Adam's apple moving up and down in a laboured manner, while his breath escaped in gasps. He began to pour sweat like he had been doused with water. After a series of gasps, he would call out in Swahili to the two young Presidential Guard Brigade (PGB) soldiers who were guarding us. *'Mtoto yangu, nimekufa.'* ['Son, I am dying.'] I feared that he was going to die right there as

54   Interview with Kesanyu (not real name), May 2009.

we watched. When the sweating became profuse and his eyes started rolling back into the sockets, one of the young men moved over and, probably fearing that the old man was indeed on his last few breaths, loosened the rope just a bit – enough to allow him breath easier, but without any possibility of movement still.

The old man and I, and ten or so other people, were lying on the floor of a garage in the Arua Presidential Lodge. The soldiers who had arrested us had a very effective method of keeping us immobile. Each person was tied up into a tight ball with very strong rope, first by securing the arms together at the back, then the ankles, and then bringing together the two ends of the rope at the back to the extent possible. The effect was that one's chest movements were very restrained, making breathing very difficult indeed. When I was brought to the garage, I had found some people already lying on the floor, and as the day progressed more people were brought in and tied in similar fashion. By nightfall there were about twenty people in all. The following morning seven more people were brought into the garage, and around midday the beatings began. It is difficult to describe the brutality of those beatings – especially as we were all tied up and lying in vulnerable positions. These beatings went on for a long while, and the soldiers kept asking us what we knew about rebellion, and if we had met with Besigye. For the next few days, we were interrogated and beaten during the day, and at night we were tied up in pairs and left to lie motionless on the floor in the mosquito-infested garage. On 25 November we were finally moved from the Presidential Lodge to the army barracks. The following day, to our surprise, we were untied and told to go out. We left the barracks building and walked outside, to be met by a shocking sight. There in the compound was a huge crowd of people, including photographers, clearly waiting to see us. Even more astonishing, right in front of us was a large collection of military equipment – different types of guns, all on display. We were told to go and sit behind the guns as the cameras flashed away. We were introduced as having been arrested in possession of the guns. After the display we were all piled up on a pick-up truck like sacs of produce – one on top of another – and we started our journey to Kampala. Our only stop was Masindi town, where again we attracted crowds as we were taken off the truck at a small restaurant. Despite the circumstances, and the fact that by now we all stunk, we were glad to have a meal, and we ate like wolves. After our lunch we were piled back onto the pickup and spent the next four or so hours – the entire trip from Masindi and Kampala – in a ceaseless downpour. When we got off the truck at Kololo Summit View, we were all numb from the cold rain and the very cramped positions in the truck. It was a miracle that we were alive and able to stand. In Kololo the beatings were equally routine, although they sometimes happened with no interrogation as such.

Often the soldiers would beat us and tell us we did not deserve to live. A soldier called Drani often led the beatings – usually accompanied by a commentary about how Museveni was a good parent, and how anyone opposing him ought to die. Sometimes he used scissors to inflict cuts on the captives. He seemed to enjoy seeing us bleed. A female Lieutenant based at Kololo was also particularly vicious – often stepping on the captives with her high heels and telling us we were going to die. Another soldier, Arnold Kajja, would use huge sticks to hit the men, and he would not stop until the sticks were in shreds. The whole time we were there we had no baths, and our meals were a special type of cuisine. The soldiers would feed us on the water they used to wash their plates after they ate. If there were leftovers we ate that as well.

We stayed at Kololo until 5 December when we were again moved, this time to the Criminal Investigation Department in Kampala, and later the same day to the Central Police Station (CPS). Now, CPS is no luxury hotel, but in comparison to Kololo it was a vacation! We had a room in which to sleep, the meals were more substantial, and the beatings were not on the menu. This lasted three days until 8 December, when we were taken to court and charged with treason. We were then remanded to Kigo prison, which marked the beginning of our lawful imprisonment. Until then we had been held in various places, and except for the CPS, all were ungazetted and away from public scrutiny.[55]

Atukunda's experience is not as rare as one would like it to be. The Uganda Human Rights Commission, a statutory organ, has recorded increasing counts of human rights abuses since it was constituted. In 2006 the commission released a report that showed worrying trends: since 1997 abuses of the right to personal liberty and freedom from torture had been escalating. They topped a long list of human rights abuses, second only to child abuse. And who was responsible for most abuses? The Uganda police and the army.

In October 2009 Asen Busingye, the police spokesperson, made an unsettling revelation. Between January and September 2009, there had been about 5000 human rights violations reported against the police, and 3000 of them had been substantiated. The officers involved either faced disciplinary action, or had been handed over for prosecution.[56] This was an average of 15 cases a day. This was the police force, in whose hands were entrusted the safety and security of Ugandans and their property.

The Museveni government had emerged from a brutal civil war during which thousands of people were killed and millions were displaced. In that conflict the NRA was fighting to oust a sitting government – one they saw as self-imposed and illegitimate because it was based on

55   Interview with Frank Atukunda, March 2009.
56   *Monitor,* 2 October 2009.

a stolen election. One could well understand the nervousness of the Museveni regime a couple of decades later, as they imagined another wave of Ugandans taking to the bush to repeat that bloody history. Museveni knew there had been enough stolen elections. He also knew better than most people that simple-looking peasants were capable of assisting a rebellion. But if he hoped to end the cycle of rebellion and to inculcate in Ugandans a culture of the rule of law, how was that going to happen by the state engaging in similar acts of lawlessness as those that characterised the former regimes?

If Jean-Paul Sartre were an employee of the Ugandan security agencies today, he would not need to edit one dot from what he said in 1963 in reference to the brutal treatment meted out by French colonisers to the Algerian 'natives': 'Our victims know us by their scars and by their chains, and it is this that makes their evidence irrefutable.'[57]

Yet from early on, Museveni was very clear about the importance of resolving governance problems as a prerequisite for dealing with other national issues. In explaining why it was important for Ugandans to sort out the question of leadership, Museveni had explained:

> There is quite a lot of misconception not only on the question of Uganda but also on many African issues. For example you hear people say that the problem of Uganda is economic disruption. That therefore what should be done for the country is to assist the regime in power so that they can restore production. But the question is: Uganda was one of the most prosperous counties in Africa comparatively.... What went wrong? Is it the economy which went wrong? Certainly not. The starting point for all this was political mismanagement. Once the political question was mishandled and people like Idi Amin came to power then the economy had to be disrupted.
>
> So what [is] the *sine-qua-non* of rehabilitating

---

57   Jean-Paul Sartre, in the preface to Franz Fanon's *Wretched of the Earth*. (Grove Press, New York 1963.)

Uganda? It is not the economic aid to Obote or to anybody. It is the solution of the political question. Once the political question is solved, it will be the basis for solving other problems, economic questions, social questions and others. Therefore, to ignore the solution of the political question which means the restoration of democracy, the restoration of human rights of the people; to ignore those and start hankering after so-called economic recovery is holding the stick from the wrong end. It will not take us anywhere. Even if the economy is restored today, tomorrow it will be disrupted. Why? Because we have people in power who are not accountable to the people.....

Therefore, the most important question on the Uganda problems is: restoration of democracy, restoration of human rights and restoration of security of the people of Uganda.[58]

On 8 June 1991, while addressing Makerere University students and staff at Freedom Square, Museveni reiterated this point:

Without democracy, you cannot, for instance, stop corruption, which is a big cancer in Africa. Some people think that dictatorial regimes can cause development in an economy, but I don't agree. Without democracy, there is no way you can bring about development because people cannot speak freely, they cannot criticize wrong programs, they cannot criticize corruption, and without criticism things are bound to rot. So the question of democracy is a vital matter indeed for Africa.

Although in his earlier days Museveni repeatedly proclaimed that governance issues were at the core of a stable and prosperous society, he seemed to have changed his mind somewhere along the

---

58   From *Selected Articles on the Uganda Resistance War* by Yoweri Museveni, 1985. Page 34

way. In 2005 when the dust settled on the debate on constitutional amendments, the most contested of which was lifting the term limits to allow him to run for office indefinitely, Museveni told journalists that they were wasting time to discuss such petty issues.

> You wasted a lot of time and power, discussing *kisanja*, *kisanja* (presidential term limits.) You get into trouble because you involve yourselves in very small and petty things. *Kisanja* was just a procedural matter. It was a means to an end, not an end in itself. Now that it is finished what will you talk about?[59]

From then on Museveni told every audience he addressed that the most important things were the economy and the poverty alleviation programme. And as had become the habit, all the Movement cadres started singing from this new chorus sheet, that talk about governance was idle and the preoccupation of the disgruntled opposition. Far from being small or petty, however, many political commentators think that the term limits constitutional amendment was one of Museveni's low moments, and that the fact that Uganda could not change leadership at that point set the country on a precipitous slope likely to lead to an entrenched dictatorship and possible armed conflict in the future. In response to demands from civil society and the political opposition for electoral reforms ahead of the 2011 elections, Museveni wished to quash all talk on governance. He especially did not want to hear this from representatives of Western governments whose budgetary support was still vital for the Ugandan economy. On 12 March 2010, while speaking at a book launch in Kampala, Museveni said, 'Donors should not tie development assistance to demands for better governance and democracy. Donor aid should come in areas where Uganda needs development, not in governance. I am already an expert in governance. Who can again lecture me on governance?'

Having talked so eloquently and convincingly about the fundamental role that democracy played in fostering development, Museveni now seemed content to receive a steady flow of donor money with his left hand, while on his right he shook hands with thieving members of his cabinet (many of who had been found guilty of serious

59   *Monitor*, 27 September 2005.

electoral offences and human rights abuses) and patted the backs of his campaign managers (who routinely bought votes, used guns to intimidate the electorate, stole public funds with impunity, and told tax payers that they would not account for the money they used to bribe Parliamentarians). Indeed, Museveni needed no lectures on governance. What he needed was someone to read to him his own writing of two decades back. It was still true that 'to ignore the solution of the political question which means the restoration of democracy, the restoration of human rights of the people; to ignore those and start hankering after so-called economic recovery is holding the stick from the wrong end'.

Courtesy *New Vision*
President Museveni donning dry banana leaves, a symbol of an additional term.

Mike Chibita, a highly respected lawyer who has served in the Ministry of Justice as well as in State House, expressed reservations about the notion that development could only come as a result of democracy.

> I have come to appreciate that there is no perfect democracy. But for this government, I think we cannot hold them up to such a high standard of democracy. As you know they started off by taking power by

undemocratic means. They overturned a constitution, and we allowed and welcomed them. Most people were okay with that. We accepted it. You know, people had been brutalized by Amin, and Obote, and we all probably thought, 'this is a revolution'. By the way, it is provided for in law – the fact that a government can change by constitutional means, or through a revolution. And once a revolution is successful, the leaders of the revolution set aside the constitution, and they put in place a new one.

So there was complicity – we all agreed to the group – the NRA – taking power through unconstitutional means. And later when a few things started to appear contradictory, most people still did not protest. You remember Wasswa Ziritwawula[60]? Back in 1994 he was the first – and at that time I think the only one – who decided to walk out of the National Resistance Council after the Council moved goal posts. [The Council extended the NRM rule by another five years without seeking the people's mandate through an election] Everyone else at that point stayed put. Maybe there were others who felt uncomfortable, but they did not speak up. So there was complicity even at that point.

Rather than looking at democracy per se, we need to look at certain parameters – the rule of law. Yes… when impunity has been eliminated, so that when people commit crimes, they are taken to court and they are tried. And that the reverse is true – that if someone has not committed a crime they should not be framed, or if they are, the system should exonerate [the innocent people]. The other one [parameter]

60   Joseph Wasswa Ziritwawula was a member of the Democratic Party. On 20 October 1989 he resigned from the National Resistance Council. He said in his resignation letter that the Resistance Movement's extension of its own mandate and the manner in which it was done were 'morally unacceptable and fundamentally undemocratic'.

is the free press. If the press is responsible and independent, they play a very big role in holding people accountable.

So – it is possible that there are other modes of governance. And the society moves ahead – that is what they say of those Asian countries – Malaysia, Indonesia, Singapore, and so on - they were not exemplary democracies, but they had a focus. Though they were not having periodic elections for the head of state, they were clear that they wanted to progress... the citizens were assured of certain freedoms. So the basic freedoms – freedom from torture, from persecution, harassment... these [practices] are unacceptable. Whether it is happening in America [or anywhere else], it is unacceptable. You can't have that. People should not be imprisoned without trial, people should not be tortured. If one is arrested they should be charged within the prescribed 48 hours, and it should be clear why they are arrested. Even those arrested on suspected terrorism – we have the terrorism law, so they can still be dealt with within the law. Because it is what is called a slippery slope – once you have tortured someone by pulling their ear, the next time you will be pulling their nose, then two people, and where does it stop? It is better if you [the country] did not get onto the slope in the first place. So if you are on the slope, at any opportune moment you should ensure that you do not continue along the slope. The sooner you ensure that you are not going down the slope the better. I cannot say the point at which we should be looking for something different – one cannot say after so many people have been killed in detention, or after so many people have been detained without trial... it is not a quantitative thing.[61]

In July 2002 the government arrested a number of opposition

---

61   Interview with Mike Chibita, October 2009.

supporters on allegations that they were engaged in rebel activity. One of those arrested was twenty-three-year-old Patrick Owomugisha Mamenero. On 23 July 2002 Mamenero died while in detention at CMI headquarters. His death certificate showed that he had died from a head injury inflicted with a blunt object. His extrajudicial killing was never investigated.

M.F. 105

UGANDA MINISTRY OF HEALTH

MEDICAL CERTIFICATE OF CAUSE OF DEATH

(Not to be used by any other than a Registered or Licensed Practitioner)

I HEREBY CERTIFY that (full name) *Owomugisha Patrick*
nationality *Ugandan* of (residence) *Kabale*
whose occupation was that of *Self employed* that such person's age
was stated to be *32* that I last saw ~~him alive~~ *him dead* on the *24th*
day of *July* *2002* that he/~~she~~ died (a) on the *23rd*
day of *July 2002* at *4.30* p.m./~~a.m.~~ at (place) *On the way to Hospital*
and that to the best of my knowledge and belief the cause of death was as hereunder stated.

Approximate interval between onset and death *Uncertain*

I Disease or condition directly leading to death (b).   (a) *Subdural haematoma*
     due to (or as a consequence of)
     (b) *Blunt injury*
     due to (or as a consequence of)

PM 139/2002

     (c)

Witness my hand this *24* day of *July* 19 *2002*

W. ABINGA H.

(a) Should the Medical Officer not feel justified in taking upon himself the responsibility of certifying the fact of death, he may here insert the words **as I am informed.**

(b) This does not mean the mode of dying, e.g. heart failure, asthenia, etc. It means the disease, injury or complication which caused death.

Mamenero death certificate

88

Around the time that Mamenero was murdered, many people who had remained active in Reform Agenda circles continued to attract unwelcome attention from the state. I had never been one to engage in politics, so after the elections I had retreated back to the hospital. Although I was not involved in politics, I was informed by a friend who worked with my Internet service provider that my e-mails were regularly monitored. I discovered that my bank accounts were under surveillance. A family friend that worked with the Movement Secretariat came to the hospital and told me that there were two informers on my staff in the casualty department. I am not sure whether this was done in the genuine belief that I was a useful source of intelligence information, or whether it was a form of subtle harassment.

One evening in May 2002, three armed men forced their way into our home, ordered our girls and I to lie face down on the laundry floor, and proceeded to take whatever valuables they wanted from the house. They loaded them in my car and drove it away. The whole operation could not have taken longer than forty minutes, but it left me badly rattled. My discomfort was not helped by the thought that I might be under some form of surveillance. Working conditions at the hospital seemed to get worse as the workload got heavier and the health sector experienced budget cuts. I started to think that a different environment might be helpful, and in 2003 I left to go and work for the United Nations in Brazzaville, Republic of Congo.

On 23 November 2004 my brother Joseph Musasizi (Saasi) was arrested and taken to the Joint Anti-Terrorism Task Force safe house in Kololo. Later he was transferred to the Central Police Station (CPS) in Kampala, then brought before court and charged with treason and concealment of treason. He was sent to Kigo prison, his first leg of what was going to be a long and tortuous journey.

Saasi had been arrested before, but on the first occasion he was interrogated, his house was thoroughly searched (while surrounded by more than fifteen heavily armed soldiers that sealed off all access to his compound and the neighbours' homes), and he was released without any charges. A couple of years prior to that arrest, when I still worked as a surgeon at Mulago Hospital, he narrowly escaped being killed in a shoot-to-kill incident whose investigation fizzled out rather abruptly. He had spent the weekend in Rukungiri driving a friend's car, but just before they left Rukungiri to head back to Kampala, Saasi returned the vehicle to its owner and followed an hour or so later in another car. The car he had been driving earlier was trailed, and when it was a few miles outside Lyantonde town the killers closed in and showered the vehicle with bullets, wounding the driver fatally. The incident took place at around two o'clock on a fine sunny afternoon. The other vehicle occupants escaped with bullet wounds. I learnt of the incident through a distress phone call from Saasi, who had rushed to Lyantonde health centre where his friend was declared dead on arrival about an hour after the shooting. For one who had experienced serious and repeated threats to his life, Saasi remained cheerful and appeared undeterred in his enjoyment of life. He seemed to have lost the idealism of youth without losing any of the vigour. In 1986 before I knew anything about the NRM's ten-point programme, Saasi was reciting all ten points, although his favourite was explaining how Uganda was going to build 'an independent, integrated, and self-sustaining national economy'. He was going to become a sunflower seed millionaire, he often told us. But while planning for the sunflowers, Saasi did many other things – he had a knack for getting things done, and he had an incredible network of friends and business colleagues. In my many moves in and out of the country, Saasi could help me to find furniture and a car, or get rid of them with impressive speed. He chaired wedding meetings and organised funerals and graduation parties. We often joked that if Saasi could not find someone's contact, then they did not exist. He was probably given to taking things too lightly and failed to appreciate the gravity of the allegations that were often levelled against him. Christine, his wife, told me of an incident that occurred several months before Saasi was arrested. She and Saasi had gone to Rukungiri for the weekend. On their way back to Kampala, they put a sack of foodstuffs in the boot of the car. They never found out whether word was sent to security operatives in Kampala or whether they were followed all the way from Rukungiri. When they finally pulled up outside their house, another vehicle pulled up behind them, and some armed people got out. They ordered Saasi to open the boot and step back. He obliged. They heaved the heavy sack out, ripped it open, and poured its contents onto the ground. When everything was out, they looked at each other, puzzled. One of them asked Saasi where he had put the guns. After the initial shock Saasi told them that he had magic – he had turned the guns into potatoes.

The day Saasi was arrested, my sister Margaret was travelling back to Kampala from a business trip in Dubai. A friend called her and told her about the arrest. They also advised her to stay away, as there was already a search out for her. Her office and home were turned upside down, and her employees were interrogated, presumably about her contacts with rebels. Later the government listed her as one of the terrorists in the great lakes region; the claim, for anyone who knew Margaret, was a hilarious joke. But the government was right in considering her dangerous – not in the violent terrorist sense, but because of two important attributes. She had a business that was making money, and she was loyal to a fault. If Reform Agenda needed to deliver campaign materials, or lawyers needed to pay for some research, and there was no source of ready cash, she could be counted on to provide it. She fuelled cars, bought food for campaigners, paid printers for campaign posters – in short, she funded activities that the Movement could not afford to see succeed. And in this Margaret was not alone, or even the most financially resourceful of supporters. There were and still are hundreds, maybe thousands of citizens that willingly put considerable personal incomes to the use of legitimate political opposition. Margaret happened to be among the more conspicuous because of her relationship with Besigye. Margaret was well acquainted with life in exile. In 1977 her father-in-law, Erinayo Oryema, was murdered by Amin, and she and her husband, William Oryema, fled into exile. She had lived in Kenya and later in the UK. When she returned to Uganda after the 1986 liberation war, she believed she would never have to leave again.

Chapter 10: Change the President, Not the Constitution

'The Resistance Movement that I have led for the last 34 years has a clear philosophy... It is: "All power belongs to the People." The framers of the 1995 Constitution (where some of us were not) should have at every turn and corner, ensured this principle. If they did not... that was their failure.' – Yoweri Museveni[62]

Talk of amending the ten-year-old constitution to lift presidential term limits started like a joke in bad taste. Many Ugandans were taken by surprise when it gained momentum, until it had overshadowed all other debate, both in the national Parliament and in the *'bimeeza'*, or the 'people's Parliament' – live radio talk shows, some of which were open-air broadcasts. In characteristic fashion, the man at the heart of the debate – in fact the only person who stood to gain from this amendment, having been in power for two consecutive terms and due to step down – initially kept quiet. Museveni let other people do the begging on his behalf. Cabinet Ministers, Members of Parliament, district leaders – all those wishing to gain from Museveni's continued rule came forth to support the 'third term' project. In fact it was not going to be a third term, since Museveni would have been in power for twenty years, equivalent to four presidential terms, and neither was the proposed amendment about one more term. It was about the removal of all terms limits. Salaam Musumba was a member of the 7th Parliament which amended the constitution, and she talked to me about her experiences of those times.

Talk of the amendment started as whispers. Even Museveni was not

---

62   Part of a response to James Wapakhabulo, former Speaker. *Monitor*, 13 May 2004.

sure how it would be received. It had been a campaign matter in 2001 by Reform Agenda, and their contention at the time was to stall Museveni's plot to change the constitution. So when it came to pass it started as whispers. Then the whispers got bolder and bolder until they became desperate. So it eventually dawned on us that what had been feared was real, and that it fell within our Parliament to deal with it. So our first struggle was to ensure that if the constitution was to be amended – especially the first amendment – it should be done constitutionally. We determined that we would not let anyone vandalise the constitution.

Musumba recounted how many Parliamentarians felt a sense of betrayal and of self-blame. There were people, she said, who truly believed that this would never happen. This included people like Henry Tumukunde, who was bewildered at the very thought.[63] The 'Historicals'[64] were wondering how the process ever got out of their hands. And how could Besigye have been so right – and with such precision? For them it was an internal struggle – their place in history, their place in society, what they had worked for, and how it had turned out. A lot of people were in paralysis. So once Museveni had garnered enough support and understood that he could control the process, the Executive came to Parliament. They approached the speaker, Francis Ayume, but he too was bewildered by the prospect of the amendment.

Musumba had been out of Parliament for four years, but she described the events as if they had occurred only a few months back. She sat across the table from me, her two cell phones out of view but not out of hearing range. She ignored them. While talking to her, I realised how different she was from the Musumba that the press liked to present. There was no extremism, no anger, and no rough edges. She spoke with conviction and clarity, and she had no problem naming names.

He [Ayume] was seen as a threat, so he was removed

_____

63   Tumukunde was forced to resign his seat in Parliament and was replaced by Brig. Andrew Gutti, who voted in favour of the bill.
64   Original members of the National Resistance Movement & Army in 1986.

and made Attorney General, and replaced with Edward Sekandi. They probably knew he could be prevailed upon. Once Parliament was attacked from the head, it became easy to handle the individual members. The first vulnerable points were the women – the women who, according to Museveni, should be eternally grateful that he brought them to the table, to the boardroom. Then they started to approach individual members though their families – their spouses, older children at college, siblings. Henry Tumukunde and Col. Fred Bogere were the only ones that stood and passed the test of history. Bogere is the biggest hero. He was a soldier under Museveni, but he stood against the vandalising of the constitution. Then there were the cheer girls. That was the beginning of the end of affirmative action because they [Executive] turned district women MPs into cheerleaders, like on a soccer field. They do not expect them to have any intellectual input.[65]

The lifting of presidential term limits became a major project for the Executive. Ministers who did not support it were summarily dropped from cabinet. These included Jaberi Bidandi Ssali, a long serving minister in the Movement and the chair of the Elect Yoweri Museveni Task Force in 2001. Others were Eriya Kategaya[66], Miria Matembe, Sarah Nakiyingi, and Amanya Mushega.

In one entertaining incident in January 2004, four cabinet ministers and some twenty-eight MPs danced and chanted slogans supporting the third term at a rally in Ssembabule district in southern Uganda. They said President Yoweri Museveni should copy other African leaders and reign for life. Then Energy Minister Saida Bbumba, the convener of the occasion to launch a rural electrification project, said former Tanzania President Julius Nyerere ruled for forty-one years, Nelson Mandela of South Africa retired at ninety, and Arap Moi of

65   Interview with Salaam Musumba, Secretary General of the Forum for Democratic Change, March 2010.
66   After Museveni's controversial win of the 2006 presidential election, Kategaya made peace with him and accepted an appointment in his cabinet.

Kenya left power at eighty-two.[67] Bbumba is reported to have said the following.

> I support Museveni to copy from Moi, consider leaders like Omar Bongo of Gabon who has been in power for over thirty-seven years, Fidel Castro of Cuba, and Muammar Gaddafi of Libya who began a revolution and even now nobody wants to remove him from power. We should copy Gaddafi because even ours is a revolution, those opposing the third term want us to lose the future development Museveni wants to fulfil.

She added that Museveni was the only one whose language was understood in Washington, where Uganda gets the funds to do work such as the rural electrification.

> Museveni has turned this wilderness [Ssembabule] into a town by installing power here. He lobbies for money from donors. Without him nothing can be achieved because all the development is attributed to him.[68]

Many of the MPs who attended the event said Museveni should rule for life or until he was too old to continue. Samuel Abura, MP for Matheniko, said they would be happy to escort a senile Museveni to Rwakitura (Museveni's village) after clocking eighty-two years, while Mike Ssebalu from Busiro East was reported to have proposed that the term limits issue be brought up at the African Parliament so that no leader is given a limit. Others said Museveni was their milk-producing cow that should not be slaughtered yet.

It was this frenzy that saw Parliamentarians being 'facilitated' with

---

67   Julius Nyerere was president of Tanzania for twenty-four years, from 1961 to 1985. Tanzania had been independent for thirty-eight years when he died at the age of seventy-seven. Kenya's Daniel arap Moi handed over power in a democratic transition when he was seventy-eight, not eighty-two. He had been president for twenty-four years. Nelson Mandela was released from prison at the age of eighty-two, and he became the first president of a democratic South Africa in 1994. He left power after one five-year term.

68   The *New Vision*, 20 January 2004.

5 million Uganda shillings each (equivalent to US$2,500 at the time), widely seen as inducement, to vote in support of lifting the term limits. John Kazoora, an NRA bush war veteran and former Member of Parliament who is now in the opposition, expressed his disillusionment with what happened:

> You can imagine the bribery of Parliament in order to change the constitution and lift term limits – one can understand a peasant taking half a kilo of salt or a piece of soap in exchange for his vote. But the MPs! Each MP gets a minimum of USh 9 million [US$4,500] per month. So what business do they have taking a bribe of 5 million to change a constitution? That was one grand opportunity that we [the country] squandered. If the Parliament had stuck to their principles and refused to change the constitution regarding term limits, that would have been an important landmark in Uganda's defence of constitutionalism. People say that maybe Museveni would have brought out the army – but that would have been another level. But now we have people in Parliament, and many in cabinet, led by a whole professor of public health,[69] who go around declaring that only one man in this country has a vision![70]

So were MPs really bribed to change the constitution? Musumba described the circumstances surrounding the USh 5 million payments.

> There was concern that the constitutional amendment discussions had been a Kampala affair, and that we needed to bring the rest of the country into

---

69   Reference to Vice President Gilbert Bukenya, a professor of public health. He attracted ridicule when he announced that he was not interested in becoming President. He sounded anxious to assure the President that he posed no political threat – a lame position for a Vice President. Prof. Bukenya was dean of the Makerere Institute of Public Health before he joined politics. Shortly after he left, Auditor General Tumwesigye found that he had stolen money from the university. He was made to refund it.

70   Interview with John Kazoora, October 2009.

the discussion. So it was decided administratively that resources should be found to facilitate Parliamentarians to go and explain to the people what was happening. But the idea was then hijacked. The 'yellow girls' took it up – Hope Mwesigye and Anifa Kawooya. They co-opted some other women. They decided that the money should be used as a reward – and to consolidate support for the Movement. We would never have known about it had [Hon. Theodore] Sekikubo, who was supposed to be one of the beneficiaries, not been denied. He was told they needed to check his credentials again. He was furious. He came back to Parliament and went public about it [the money]. Olive Wonekha was under the table counting the money. Mwesigye was administering the money, and Kawooya was ensuring that people signed before receiving the cash. The manner in which the money was disbursed was a first for Parliament. They had a list of Movement and Movement leaning MPs, so they followed them up very closely to ensure that they did not change their minds. When they suspected that an MP was still uneasy about it [the amendment lifting term limits] they gave them a trip outside the country to ensure they would be away at the time of voting. And the fact that some MPs were away at that critical time smacked of irresponsibility. But all was not lost. What we had achieved was to bring it [amendment] in the ambit of the law. At least then the fault lines would be in Parliament. If we lost in Parliament, we still would have managed to get it done constitutionally.

Musumba had no kind words for the Speaker, who she said was a willing victim.

We needed numbers to safeguard the constitution. But the more we appeared determined to safeguard it, the more they [Executive] went for the soft targets. That was now not institutional failure; it was personal failure to stand up for Uganda. The Speaker of Parliament Sekandi was the worst enemy of the constitution. He surrendered. He could not withstand pressure, but he also lent himself to compromise. Jacob Oulanyah [Chair, Committee on Legal and Parliamentary Affairs] was also lacking in principle. When the hour of testing came he failed his own test. He was willing to be the Judas. He wrote a minority report to cover himself but he had been reported in private meetings with the Executive, had been pampered, his ego had been inflated, and after the task he was discarded. He did not read history well, and he became history himself.

In all fairness many people are still failing to read history and to accept its meaning even when laid out plainly. On 12 February 2008 at Kyeizooba in East Bushenyi, Museveni could not have talked more plainly when he explained why he was not planning to retire. '*Niinye nahiigire enyamaishwa yange nkagiita. Mbwenu ngu ngyende! Nzehi?*' 'It is I who went hunting, and after killing my animal some people want me to go. Where should I go?'[71] The answer to the rhetorical question should probably have been, 'Nowhere. All power belongs to the hunter.' That is why Museveni found the constitution, with its reference to presidential term limits, very inconvenient.

Salaam Musumba told me what she thought happened to some of the older people who supported the lifting of presidential term limits: 'People could recall Amin, they could recall Obote.... But they remained so focused on the driving mirror; they did not look in the windscreen. They were too preoccupied with history. So they looked at history and they were paralysed. That is what happened in our time.'

The presidential term limits debate reminded one of a common practice in surgery. In order to successfully complete a major operation of the abdomen, surgeons usually need to place sutures or staples to hold the edges of the wound together. If this were not

71   *Monitor,* 14 February 2008.

done, the wound would gape and the abdominal contents would begin to pour out as soon as the patient got up; the pain would be unbearable. Even with good pain control, this state of affairs would not be compatible with normal healing. So the sutures play a crucial role: they maintain the integrity of the wound and abdomen, they stop bleeding, and they reduce the chances of infection. In a few hours healing is well underway. But indispensable as the sutures may be, after five to seven days they need to be removed. If they are left in place, the same body that would have perished without them will begin to reject them. The body recognizes them as being foreign. Germs begin to use their presence to cause trouble in the otherwise nicely healing wound. The tissue around the sutures begins to rot. If the offending sutures are still left in place, the wound begins to ooze pus. At some point the suture material may work itself loose and get expelled with the pus, leaving a chronic wound and ugly scars. Once the sutures have done their job, the best thing that can happen is not to allow them extra time because they were so useful at the beginning; it is to take them out and let the body get on with healing itself. It would be strange to find a group of surgeons debating the merits and demerits of removing sutures from a healing wound.

Chapter 11: Trials on the Trail

'The state should guarantee security of person and property. If it does not do that, why should people owe it allegiance?' – Yoweri Museveni[72]

In 2005 the Museveni camp seemed confident in their knowledge that Besigye would not be on the 2006 ballot paper. He was living in exile in South Africa, and the assumption was probably that some other candidate would be picked to run against the incumbent. Then talk of Besigye's return started. The weeks leading to his return were packed with speculation: some people thought he could not possibly return to Uganda – and to certain imprisonment. From my base in Brazzaville, I followed the events by phone and by Internet news. Forum for Democratic Change leaders in Kampala had held a number of meetings with Besigye in South Africa, and homecoming preparations were underway in Uganda. A week or so to the anticipated departure, I called and talked to Besigye and asked if he was really going home. He said yes without hesitation. We were on one hand excited about what that could mean politically, and on the other very afraid for his safety. The day came – slowly it seemed, but it did come. He eventually left South Africa after nearly four years in exile. The return party went through Nairobi, where they were joined by his wife, Winnie, and son, Anselm, before getting onto the final leg for Entebbe.

In Uganda the mood amongst his supporters was one of celebration, victory, and defiance all in one. The government stance was a mixture of calculated inattention (let him come; he is irrelevant) and

---

72   Yoweri K. Museveni, 'Political Substance and Political Form', *What Is Africa's Problem?* (University of Minnesota Press, 2000).

watchful hostility. The whole airport area was cordoned off at dawn, and vehicles were not allowed through the wide-radius security ring that had been put up to discourage people from receiving Besigye at Entebbe. But the plan was leaked in the night by some security personnel sympathetic to the political reform cause. Subsequently many of Besigye's supporters managed to get to Entebbe before the road blocks went up. The blockade only served to heighten the anticipation and to turn what should have been a huge and chaotic crowd at the airport into a grand homecoming parade, with masses of people lined up all the way from Entebbe to Kampala. Having failed to keep the people away, the government responded by deploying the police and military all along the twenty-two-mile stretch from the airport to Kampala.

Besigye was returning to a situation that was in many ways very different from that which he had left in 2001. His wife and young son were now resident in Ethiopia, where Winnie had taken up a job at the African Union. His young brother Saasi had been in prison for a year, and all his sisters had left the country: Margaret had run into exile, Stella had moved back to the UK, and I had left the country to go and work for the United Nations. Many close relatives had taken a low profile to survive. A number of friends and colleagues who had stood with him in 2001 had died, including Spencer Tirwomwe. Some, like Anne Mugisha, had gone into exile. Others, like Winnie Babihuga, had taken up international jobs and left the country, while others joined the Movement. But rather than being beaten down, the opposition had continued to grow. Although still very restricted in their activities, the political parties had managed to widen the political space, in no small measure courtesy of the Democratic Party, which tirelessly challenged the government's unconstitutional practices in court. The Elect Kizza Besigye Task Force of 2001 had morphed into Reform Agenda, and with the infusion of more political actors, a new party, the Forum for Democratic Change, had been born. People who had not been involved in politics before 2000, like Beti Kamya, threw themselves into building the party with zeal.

A key factor in determining the timing of Besigye's return was the deadline for registration of candidates. The government had relied on this as a legal and easy way to keep him out of the presidential race. Now he had returned, and for the next few weeks Besigye took the country by storm. Everywhere he went there were the same massive, enthusiastic crowds that had turned up on his campaign trail four years previously. Voter registration, which had been lukewarm, suddenly picked up as people, particularly the youth, rushed to get their voters' cards. Besigye's visits were comprehensively covered in the media. This did nothing to endear him to the Movement government – it was certainly not helped by the fact that on a number of occasions during his speeches, he dared the government to arrest him if they had a case against him.

Then one day they did. Even the most ardent supporters of the Museveni regime would probably agree that if the police had set out to pick the worst possible timing and location to arrest Besigye, they succeeded.

Kampala is a city chocked from too many vehicles and not enough road space. The mix of vehicles is unbelievable – huge trucks carrying construction materials jostle for space with the latest models of sleek European and Japanese cars. There is no place for the traffic to go when emergency vehicles need clear passage. In March 2009 the biggest market in Kampala caught fire, and a fair portion of it was razed to the ground. It was located less than 500 meters from the central fire station, but the traffic jam was so dense that the fire engines could not access the burning market. It was in the midst of such traffic that the Besigye arrest was conducted.

Besigye was on his way back into Kampala after a series of crowd-drawing rallies in western Uganda, all of which had been covered in the media. His motorcade had come down the road that runs west to east along the southern boundary of the city, and it was right in the middle of dense and slow midafternoon Kampala traffic when policemen emerged by the side of his vehicle and ordered him to come out of the vehicle. One would think that the armed forces had had enough encounters with the man to know that he would do no such thing without a fight. Thanks to the ubiquitous cell phone, within minutes the whole city and country knew that Besigye was being arrested; the news must have reached a dozen or so cities around the world. My sister Margaret, then resident in southern Africa, sent me a text message on my cell phone simply saying, 'KB arrested!' The FM radios were talking to his lawyers and to members of his delegation, and all this was being relayed live on various radio stations.

Spontaneous demonstrations broke out and then rapidly degenerated into violent riots. The city was soon engulfed in tear gas and the sound of gunfire. When all this died down, Besigye was in custody. He was to be charged with treason and rape, offences that carried a death sentence; therefore bail could not be granted until after six months. That was 14 November 2005, one month to the presidential nominations.

The 2006 political campaigns threw the entire country into hysterical spasms of electioneering. The presidential and parliamentary polls were to be held on the same day, so the constituencies were hives of frenzied activity. Reports of intimidation and violence were commonplace. Calls for civility and order by the Electoral Commission, widely thought to be partisan, were ignored.

Besigye's candidacy appeared doomed because he was clearly going to be safely behind bars when the nomination of presidential candidates took place on 14–15 December 2005. The government stated that he could not be nominated in absentia. The FDC maintained that there was nothing in the law to prevent a candidate from being nominated via a proxy. The Electoral Commission asked the Attorney General to give his legal opinion regarding the nomination of a candidate in absentia.

'I note that you do not mention the case of Dr. Kizza Besigye,' responded Attorney General Professor Khiddu Makubuya. 'Your letter is unlikely to have arisen because of the other twenty-nine prospective Presidential Candidates. Only one of the prospective Presidential Candidates is likely to have problems with physical presence for the purpose of nomination.' Then came the opinion:

> Anybody aspiring to occupy the office of President which is the highest office in the land and is the embodiment of a sovereign state should be a person of

integrity, of high moral values and be law abiding.... His conduct is a subject of serious criminal proceedings. Although he is presumed innocent until proved guilty, it certainly cannot be said that he is on the same level of innocence as that of the other Presidential Candidates. Even if he is blameless, he is currently a subject of serious charges of treason and concealment of treason in the High Court....

It is my considered opinion that Dr. Besigye's nomination would at this point in time, be tainted with illegalities. His nomination should therefore not proceed. If the Commission feels strongly that in its view he deserves to be nominated it should defer consideration of the decision to accept his nomination until after his trial in the appropriate Court has been completed.[73]

Khiddu Makubuya's opinion was given on 7 December, a week before the nominations. Even if the High Court had suspended all other business to deal with Besigye's cases, it was not feasible that they could conclude them within that time.

From any other legal mind, the above opinion might have attracted surprise. From Makubuya it had an additional twist. In 1987, when Museveni set up the Commission of Inquiry into Violations of Human Rights that had occurred between independence in 1962 and the commencement of Museveni's reign in 1986, Makubuya, then an associate professor of law at Makerere University, was appointed as a Commissioner. When the report was finally submitted, Makubuya held certain differing views that were not easily reconcilable with those of the other Commissioners, and he submitted a minority report to address those issues. One of them was the presumption of innocence. This is what he wrote at the time:

We need to categorise crimes and apply the presumption of innocence peculiarly to specific categories: (a)

---

73   Attorney General's correspondence MJ/AG/120, 7 December 2005, addressed to the Chairman Electoral Commission.

> Political crime, e.g. treason, sedition, levying war, etc.
> Since these ordinarily involve contests for power, political
> expression and struggle for participation in governance,
> suspects in respect of such offences need to be entitled
> to an unqualified presumption of innocence.

With Besigye's nomination hanging in the balance, fate had handed Makubuya the perfect opportunity to make his strong opinions count. What he told the Electoral Commission stood in stark contrast to his earlier convictions.

It seemed that if Makubuya's opinion was to be accepted, not only would Besigye not get listed on the ballot, but in the future all the state had to do to keep a troublesome politician from an election was to arrest them before nomination. Thankfully for Besigye and future leaders, the Minister of State for Justice and Constitutional Affairs, Hon. Adolf Mwesige, gave a differing opinion.

> As long as a person satisfies the requirements/quali-
> fications set out… that person can stand for election
> as President or Member of Parliament, even if he/she
> has been charged, provided that he/she has not been
> convicted and sentenced for a period exceeding nine
> months without an option of a fine. In my view there
> is no legal bar to prevent Dr. Kizza Besigye from
> being nominated as a presidential candidate.

Another hurdle had been overcome. Those close to Besigye, like Winnie Byanyima, Beti Kamya, Sam Njuba, and Obeid Kamulegeya, had had little sleep as they moved from lawyers' chambers to court, from Luzira Prison to media houses, in a do-or-die effort to secure the nomination. Not only were they battling Besigye's continued imprisonment, but there were reports that some people in government were secretly encouraging the FDC to front an alternative candidate. When Besigye finally got released on bail, he split his time between the numerous court appearances and the campaign trail.

David Mpanga recalled what it was like for Besigye's legal defence team.

The rape trial started on 2 January 2006. Besigye was being guarded like a dangerous animal. Armed guards in the windows, entire blocks cordoned off. Initially we were not allowed access to our client. When we finally got to talk to him we were denied access to some of the important documents for the case. Then it turned out that the [police] statement from the complainant had been taken in State House - in the residence of the one person most interested in Besigye's conviction. The state's key witness [Besigye's housemaid] had been abducted and imprisoned on the orders of CID chief Elizabeth Kutesa, to compel her to testify. She was being provided for by the state, which had got her a house, as well as started and financed a chicken business for her. Mama Malita, Besigye's adopted mother from the bush days, who had since the beginning of Besigye's political troubles been taken wholly under the wing of State House, was brought to testify against him. Prosecution called her as a witness although she had nothing meaningful to add to the case, except to say that she had brought the housemaid to Besigye's house. Then Elizabeth Kutesa, head of the CID, was called as a state witness. Her cross-examination revealed that the state had blatantly falsified police records. It became very clear that this case was about malicious character assassination aimed at discrediting and smearing Dr. Besigye. The state was not interested in justice.

This case was for me the final straw – to show that this here is a game. The law and the idea of the rule of law are necessary only to propagate a certain personal end – if one could do without it one would have very happily done without it. But one can't. One needs that kind of panoply to say, 'Here, we have a constitution, we have freedoms.' Freedoms mean nothing when, if it comes to something that one man thinks should not happen it does not happen. Look, we had court orders – and the court orders became [as good as] toilet paper.[74] That situation should have been completely untenable and unthinkable – but it happened. Everybody saw it. There were situations when [armed] people came to the court to physically disrupt the rule of law – the court sieges – not once but twice. The first one was on 17 November 2005, and the second one in March 2007.[75]

Courtesy *New Vision*

On 17 November 2005, these men armed with assault rifles and shot guns stormed the grounds of the High Court and attempted to take by force suspects who were being given bail from the grounds of the court. The armed men were identified as members of the UPDF Joint Anti-terrorism Task Force, Urban Hit Squad. On account of their dress, they were referred to as the Black Mambas.

In his ruling on the rape case, Justice Katutsi commented thus: 'The evidence before this court is inadequate even to prove a debt, impotent

---

74   On at least four occasions the High Court ordered the PRA suspects to be produced in court, but the orders were ignored by the prison's authorities. The suspects were never produced in court until the Solicitor General applied for a review of their bail terms.

75   Interview with David Mpanga, December 2009.

to deprive a man of his civil rights, ridiculous for convicting of the pettiest offence, scandalous if brought forward to support a charge of any character, monstrous if to ruin the honour of a man who offered himself as a candidate for the highest office in the country. I find that prosecution has dismally failed to prove its case against the accused.'

Then he added that the manner in which investigations were conducted and carried out was 'crude and amateurish and betrays the intentions behind this case'.

The intentions behind the case continued with no remorse. Besigye had so far jumped the hurdles of a registration deadline, nomination while in custody, and rape charges, but he was still spending a considerable amount of time in court rooms on the treason case when he should have been on the campaign trail. The violence that accompanied his tours was unprecedented. In one particularly tragic incident, Special Police Constable Ramathan Magara shot at a crowd of Besigye supporters that had come to wave to him at Mengo, Kampala (the seat of the Buganda Kingdom), killing two persons instantly. A third man was injured in the back and became paralysed from the waist down.[76]

---

76   Magara was protected from prosecution until 2009, when a lot of pressure from civil society resulted in his trial. He was given a fourteen-year jail sentence for manslaughter. This sparked a spontaneous protest by civil society activists outside the court. They said the sentence was not commensurate with the crime.

Courtesy James Akena

On 15 February 2006, presidential candidate Dr. Kizza Besigye went to Mengo,
the seat of Buganda kingdom, to pay a courtesy visit to the Buganda Prime
Minister. A crowd of Besigye supporters gathered around to wave to him.
Special Police Constable Magala opened fire at the crowd of unarmed civilians
and killed this man, whose body remained on the ground when the terrified
crowd fled the scene of the shooting. A second man was also fatally injured, and
a third was left quadriplegic.

One week before the polls, I returned home from Brazzaville to lend what moral support I could to my brother and his team in the dying days of the campaign. I arrived in Kampala in the midafternoon and was immediately struck by the number of posters and election materials that were on display. T-shirts, caps, car stickers, leaflets, and posters of all sizes were everywhere. There were life-size effigies of candidates Besigye and Museveni at road junctions. There was a bigger-than-life effigy of Besigye outside the FDC office on Entebbe Road. Pick-up trucks pulled life-size posters of Museveni along the streets on wheels, and noise emanating from the different camps' loudspeakers was deafening.

I went to Besigye's house in the evening and sat up till around midnight, when he eventually came in from rallies in the Kasese area. Even at that hour there were people waiting to talk to him. He did not see the last person till around one o'clock, and then he told the drivers to be ready to leave for Eastern Uganda at 5.00 AM. As he turned to go to his room, finally alone and allowing himself to let his shoulders drop, he caught sight of me, seated in a corner of the dining room. First he blinked, maybe thinking he was beginning to see visions. Then he looked again, and his face suddenly lit up. I got up to give him a hug. His fatigue left him momentarily, and I thought he was going to cry from the sheer relief and joy of seeing me there. We had not seen each other since the beginning of the campaigns, and phone calls had become increasingly difficult because of his itinerary. I was probably one of a small group of people that wanted to see him for his own sake. His reaction at seeing me brought it home to me how lonely it could be on a crowded campaign trail.

Once again, Kampala was caught up in election madness. In the sweltering heat and endless clouds of dust the usually impeccably dressed politicians climbed down from their air-conditioned four-wheel-drive vehicles, and allowed their expensive colognes to mix with the smell of sweat from the crowds of voters on the streets. *Boda bodas* (commercial motorcyclists) were doing brisk business. With candidates' posters and tree branches decorating their machines, they leaped and dodged like crazed men, weaving in and out of traffic as they raced from one rally to the next. There was no telling whether the guys you saw ahead of Museveni's motorcade this afternoon were not the same ones that led Besigye's the previous day. Few people were talking about lack of health care or the dismal quality of education. The *boda boda* cyclists were certainly not asking why Kampala city had no decent public transportation system. Once again there were threats and insults being traded in the press.

On 23 February 2006, Ugandans went to the polls in what was said to be one of the most intensely contested elections in Uganda's history.

Reminiscent of the 2001 election, the Electoral Commission made it difficult for the agents of opposition candidates to look out for the interests of their candidates. Agents of opposition parties were denied access to the tally centre to witness the tallying of the votes. Reports of rigging, vote stuffing, voter intimidation, and harassment were rampant. The *Monitor* newspaper had announced that their field reporters would phone in results from polling stations as the vote counting progressed, and that the paper would use these reports to keep a running tally on a wide screen accessible to the public. The government ordered them to cancel the show, and just to make sure that the results were not publicised, the government jammed the *Monitor* radio (KFM) signal and blocked the paper's Web site. Internal Affairs Minister Ruhakana Rugunda confirmed government interference but assured the *Monitor*'s Managing Director Conrad Nkutu that this would be short-lived. Electoral Commission Chairman Badru Kiggundu said no other centres were allowed to release results. Kiggundu could have been reading from Paulo Muwanga's script of 1980, when he told the nation that only his Military Commission could announce election results.

Two days after the poll, the Commission started announcing results without the bulk of the tally sheets from the districts. By early evening it was evident that Museveni would be announced the winner. The sense of despair was palpable among Besigye's supporters. Those of us who had been at the FDC's tally centre over the preceding two days went to Besigye's house to brief his team. We had rather patchy results except for the urban centres, the north, and Buganda. We were encouraged to keep punching in the results from our agents despite the Electoral Commission's announcements, but it was difficult to keep up morale after the definitive declaration of Museveni as the winner. Most people had not had much sleep, and they felt this was a futile exercise. Besigye was putting on a brave face, though he must have felt even more frustration that the rest of us. Winnie had come home, and she and her sisters, Martha and Edith, were at the house. The crowds had melted away, and only a few Task Force members, close friends, and one or two other relatives were present. We all sat in his living room and watched the function as the Electoral Commission made the announcements. At around 10.00 PM, I left to go back to my place. From Mbuya all the way into town and up to Kibuli, the city could have been in mourning. The only other traffic was military trucks. It was an eerie feeling, made even more so in comparison to the noise that had reigned over Kampala the previous several days. It was only in Kibuli that I found a small band of people celebrating Museveni's victory. Elsewhere people seemed to have recoiled into their shells. FDC rejected the results and lodged a petition in the courts.

Yusuf Nsibambi, a lawyer for the petition, described to me how things went during the petition hearing:

> In the 2006 presidential election petition the government realised that we had a lot of solid evidence, and even with their strong legal team they were worried. When we presented the evidence from Mbarara military barracks [where the voting process was not observed by the public] and from Katuntu's constituency, the state started hunting down witnesses and threatening lawyers.
>
> There was a soldier [Allan Barigye] from Mbarara who swore an affidavit in support of the petition. He testified about the systematic rigging within the barracks. The lawyers for the respondents [Museveni and the Electoral Commission] said they wanted to cross examine him. We brought him to court but before he got out of the car it became evident that there were soldiers all over the place waiting to

arrest him at the court. We decided to let him stay in the car. He was not cross examined. Later he was arrested and taken to a safe house. I do not know if he is alive.[77]

We decided that we would rather lose those good affidavits that endanger the witnesses' lives, because it was clear that they would be arrested. In fact even without presenting them for cross examination some of them were hunted down. The threats were very common, particularly where we insisted on tally sheets and specific polling stations where we wanted DR (Declaration of Results) forms. [We knew] where there had been no tallying, or where they could not reconcile the results with the voters' register. We put in an application for the production of specific tally sheets. The next day the lawyers [for the respondents] came back to court and said they did not have the tally sheets. The Electoral Commission officials said they had them but had not brought them to court. The records are clear. The law is clear on what is needed to get the final tally. The election results had been declared without any proof. Someone would call in from, say, Kasese, or send a fax claiming that Museveni had so many votes, and Besigye had so many. Even after the election, they could not produce the tally sheets to defend the figures. We said we wanted to look at the documents they [Electoral Commission officials] were reading from when they provided the results from the districts. We had gone through a production or discovery process which is allowed under the law. The state realized that the results were not defensible, and those Tally Sheets

---

77   *Monitor* 7, April 2006. Soldiers were particularly vulnerable to intimidation during elections. Private Bernard Tumwesigye of the Mbarara barracks reported that he refused to engage in multiple voting for Museveni. He was put in detention. In April 2006 he was shot in the abdomen, allegedly while trying to escape. He was admitted to Mbarara Hospital but was still under military detention.

would have been damning evidence. For instance the Masaka district election results were not tallied by the time we went to court. They were probably never tallied. The returning officer failed to produce the tally sheet. He said he was threatened. The court process was a mockery.

In the presidential election petition, the Supreme Court ruling stated in part:

> We find that there was non-compliance with the provisions of the Constitution, Presidential Elections Act and the Electoral Commission Act, in the conduct of the 2006 Presidential Elections, by the 1st Respondent [Electoral Commission] in the following instances:
>
> (a) in disenfranchisement of voters by deleting their names from the voters register or denying them the right to vote.
>
> (b) in the counting and tallying of results

We find that there was non-compliance with the principles laid down in the Constitution, the Presidential Elections Act, and the Electoral Commission Act in the following areas:

> (a) the principle of free and fair elections was compromised by bribery and intimidation or violence in some areas of the country.
>
> (b) the principles of equal suffrage, transparency of the vote, and secrecy of the ballot were undermined by multiple voting, and vote stuffing in some areas.

The judges then added that they were constrained to comment on four matters which had given them grave concern:

> - the continued involvement of the security forces in the conduct of elections where they have committed acts of intimidation, violence and partisan harassment;
> - the massive disenfranchisement of voters by deleting

their names from the voters' register, without their
knowledge or being heard;

- the apparent partisan and partial conduct by some
  electoral officials; and

- the apparent inadequacy of voter education.

They further noted, 'with dismay the failure of the 1st Respondent
[Electoral Commission] to avail to the Court reports of Returning
Officers on the ground that they were not available yet it is
mandatory for Returning Officers to transmit such reports to the
1st Respondent.' This last observation admitted in effect that that
the results that were announced could not be said to represent the
true outcome of the polls since they were not based on the returns
from the polling stations.

Having noted all of what went wrong with the election, the judges
still ruled by a majority of four to three to uphold the results of the
election. There was a loud echo from the 1980 election monitoring
group.

Chapter 12: How Much Does Your Vote Cost?

'There are now people of presidential calibre and capacity who can take over when I retire, and I shall be among the first to back them.' Yoweri Museveni[78]

To many Ugandans, particularly in the rural areas, elections now signal the arrival of money and all sorts of other inducements. It has become a whole economy.

'In villages votes do not cost very much money – five hundred or even two hundred shillings [equivalent to 25 and 10 American cents respectively],' Paul Kahiigi, a political activist and former LCIII (subcounty) Chairman in Bushenyi, Western Uganda, told me.

> The Movement dispatches vehicles to go around ferrying people to polling stations. Once the people get into the vehicles the buying begins. Usually the buying agents have a lot of cash in form of coins. To ensure that the people who get money deliver the votes, they insist that a Movement agent at the station votes on their behalf. In the 2006 election a minister who was running for Parliament went to Bushenyi Centenary and Stanbic Banks and withdrew a huge sum of money in coins. The money was being moved in sacks. When those banks did not have or would not give him any more coins he went to Mbarara. Someone at a bank in Mbarara called

---

78   Yoweri Kaguta Museveni, 'Building a Democratic Future', *Sowing the Mustard Seed* (London & Basingstoke: Macmillan Publishers Ltd, 1997).

us to say that the same minister had just withdrawn money in coins – we knew this [money] was going to the village voters. In some villages like Kyeitembe and Nyakabirizi cows were slaughtered, and everyone who accepted to vote for the Movement was given a kilo of meat. For people who could not afford meat this was very good inducement.[79]

In addition to being against the law, there was something vulgar about this blatant commercialisation of elections by a regime that had come to power on the ticket of clean leadership. Kahiigi talked of instances where candidates were offered large sums of money to pull out of races in order to leave only NRM candidates in the contest. Once this became known, others would declare intentions to run so that they too could be 'bought out' of the running. According to Kahiigi, this went on right up to the polls. But the peasant voters did not see the millions – theirs was a much cheaper market.

Ingrid Turinawe, another political activist from Rukungiri, described similar situations.

People get surprised that a person in the village can sell their vote for a small amount of salt. But it is true. There are many families who cannot afford salt. They have to work a full day in someone else's garden in order to get half a kilo of salt. If 'free' salt is given to them on the eve of elections, and they are told that the computer in the ballot box will see how they vote, they are going to vote as directed. Urban people do not understand this, but it is the reality in many villages.

It is these revelations that have generated cynicism, with some people now convinced that the Museveni government is not interested in poverty reduction. The grinding poverty that causes a full-grown man or woman to sell their vote for a small amount of salt seems to work well for the ruling party. Many think it is not in their interest to change it.

---

79   Interview with Paul Kahiigi, April 2009.

Kahiigi described other ways in which the ruling party candidates influences the vote.

> The Movement made very many false promises. For instance Richard Nduhura told people in Bumbire that he was bringing electricity to the villages. Electric poles were brought and deposited at intervals along the road. The people were told that if they voted for Nduhura, he would 'bring' electricity. After the election a truck came and picked up the poles, and that was the end of that project.

Richard Nduhura was not new to election meddling. In 2001 he contested for a parliamentary seat against Reform Agenda's Spencer Tirwomwe. Nduhura's agents were engaged in gross electoral malpractices, including multiple voting, underage voting, ballot stuffing, and bribery of voters. Nduhura was found to have voted for himself twice. After a court petition the election was annulled and a by-election was called. Under the prevailing electoral laws, being a proven vote thief did not bar him from running again, and he won the by-election. Museveni then appointed him to cabinet, perhaps to a ministry where integrity was not considered essential – the Ministry of Trade & Industry.

In many places the 2006 parliamentary elections encountered the same challenges as the presidential election. One example was the contest between Abdu Katuntu and Kirunda Kivejinja in Bugweri, Busoga. Kivejinja was the NRM candidate, and opposition candidate Katuntu was running on the FDC ticket. At the conclusion of the poll, Kivejinja was announced the winner. Katuntu filed a petition to annul the election. The court heard that Kivejinja deployed a squad of armed men who were under the command of one Lt. Mulindwa, alias 'Surambaya', who, according to witnesses, wrecked havoc in the constituency by harassing, torturing and intimidating Katuntu's supporters. Kivejinja then deployed another group led by one Major Kiswiriri, who canvassed the constituency addressing gatherings and telling voters that if they voted for Katuntu, they would face the entire wrath of the army.

Several of Katuntu's agents were arrested on the eve of polling day. They were physically assaulted and then dumped at Busembatya Police Post. Some were detained at Kivejinja's house. They were released on polling day after the close of the poll, with no charges or explanation. Those who had sustained serious injuries were given police forms to go to the hospital for treatment. In one parish, working through one of his agents, Kivejinja was reported to have recruited '18 strong bodied men' and 'told them that their assignment was to block Katuntu from campaigning in their village and to make life hard for him in whatever manner'. One of the men who accepted to testify said the leader was paid USh 10,000 (US$5.00) per day while the others were paid USh 3,000 (US$1.50) per day.

In another incident at Ibaako, Kivejinja, accompanied by men armed with AK-47 rifles, stopped Katuntu's campaign vehicle. They ordered the driver to get out of the vehicle and lie face down in the road. Kivejinja took away the vehicle keys from him. The driver was beaten and kicked by the armed men. The armed men emptied his pockets of all his money and then dumped him and his passengers at Iganga Police Station. There were police records of these incidents. A man who had allowed Katuntu to rent office space from him for the campaign was attacked and beaten. His assailants told him that he was very foolish to have given an office to Katuntu.

In summarising the petition judgment, the court stated in part:

> The evidence shows that there was an extraordinarily high level of intimidation, violence and torture. It was very well organised and executed by groups trained and deployed purposely to do so. The first respondent [Kivejinja] was at the heart of it. Much of it was carried out in his very presence. At times by him, or at his orders. Part of his home was turned into an illegal detention centre for those known or suspected not to be his supporters. Gangs, armed with guns and sticks, in the names of *Black Mambas* scavenged the constituency, beat and intimidated hundreds of voters cowering them to support the first respondent or punishing them for supporting the petitioner.

Many were dumped at police stations after torture and mistreatment, most likely to justify the torture and mistreatment, or to temporarily disable them and prevent them from carrying out any activity in the campaign arena. The Police itself appears to have been overwhelmed and perplexed with those events. Scores of persons were dumped at their posts and stations within the constituency mainly by the armed supporters of the first respondent [Kivejinja] from various parts of the constituency. The Police charged none of them with any offences. They merely recorded statements, issued victims with Police Form 3 and released them to go and nurse their injuries.

Then, almost as though the judges were pained and overwhelmed by what they had heard and seen, they added:

Court has already come to the conclusion that there was widespread intimidation, violence and torture of the Petitioner's supporters and agents. An election does not constitute a war of guns and sticks. It is a civic activity. It hinges upon the central concepts of freedom and fairness which constitute a constitutional norm under Article 61 of the Constitution. The totality of the evidence on record supports the conclusion that the first respondent [Kivejinja] ran his election campaign as if it was a war. He did so to the extent of even establishing or allowing the establishment of a detention room in his home for those he wanted to force into supporting him…. the overall quality of the election was so low that the election cannot qualify as free and fair.

The election was annulled and a by-election was called. Katuntu won.[80] Kivejinja retained his post as Third Deputy Prime Minister and Minister of Information and National Guidance. In 2009 he was appointed as Minister of Internal Affairs, putting him in charge of the police and prisons.

80   Abdu Katuntu v. Ali Kirunda Kivejinia and the Electoral Commission, Electoral Petition no. 7 of 2006, High Court of Uganda.

Courtesy *The Monitor*
10 March 2006. Armed men at a polling station in Kamwokya, a Kampala
suburb. While some are easily identifiable as belonging to a paramilitary group,
the Local Defence Unit, others are in plain clothes and are wielding firearms in
full view of the voters.

Courtesy *The Monitor*
In April 2007 a new breed of plain-clothes operatives emerged on Kampala streets. Wielding big sticks, they would pour onto the streets, often from around the Central Police Station, and would sometimes work alongside the police in violently dispersing demonstrators.

Chapter 13: You Are Freed in Order to Stay in Jail

'As soon as NRM takes government, not only will the state inspired violence disappear, but so will even criminal violence. Given democracy at the local level, a politicized army and police and absence of corruption at the top as well as interaction with the people, even criminal violence can disappear.

We are convinced that some of the post-independent African leaders are the ones that are just hopelessly out of depth and have got to look for scapegoats. Africa, since independence, has been tossed between, on the one hand idiotic quislings that are mere 'caricatures' of the worst aspects of the European middle class and, on the other hand, muddle-headed 'revolutionary' ideologies of Fabians, murderers and a variety of other opportunists, who spent more time putting people in preventive detention, when they are not murdering them … That is why African independence has almost begun to look as if it is a non-viable proposition.' – Yoweri Museveni[81]

The idea of preventive detention that Museveni found completely unacceptable in 1985 is both interesting and dangerous. While it might sound logical that a responsible government should preempt mischief, it carries with it the subtle suggestion that the detention could be done without due process. Museveni was right to condemn such practice and was well placed to do so, having been Minister of Defence in one of the notorious post-independent governments.

Darius Tweyambe was in preventive detention for some time and considers himself very fortunate to have survived it. He runs a stationery shop in Rukungiri town, but he had different career plans

---

81   Yoweri Museveni, *Selected Articles on the Uganda Resistance War*, 1985.

in the days before his detention. He is always very well turned out, if a trifle too formally for someone in his occupation. When not in a tie and jacket, he will don a very smart Kaunda suit. His language is that of one who enjoys formal speech. He does not talk in generalities; his detailed account gives the impression that he has thought a lot about his recent experiences and has them nicely catalogued under his neat hair cut.

From the days when Besigye left the army and decided to contest for the presidency some of us have had many problems – we have been oppressed, beaten, tortured and imprisoned. In 2001 during the campaigns, the Presidential Protection Unit was posted here [in Rukungiri] headed by Capt. Ndahura. I recall when Salim Saleh[82] came here to campaign for his brother, I was beaten in the stadium by Capt Ndahura in full view of everyone. I reported the case to the police, but he was never called to answer. The case was not followed up.

During the local council elections, I campaigned for the position of District Youth Councillor here in Rukungiri. I had a lot of support from the people. We were three candidates – a teacher in Ndama subcounty; Ngabirano Emmy, who was political assistant to Jim Muhwezi;[83] and myself. Letters were

---

82   Salim Saleh, alias Caleb Akandwanaho. He is Museveni's young brother. He is a bush war veteran and has held many senior positions in the army and in government, including that of Minister of State for Microfinance. He gained notoriety over a number of high-profile business scams, including the sale of Uganda Commercial Bank and the purchase of junk helicopters for the army. He confessed to having taken a bribe over the helicopter deal and was pardoned by Museveni, who told him to use the bribe money on projects in war-ravaged northern Uganda (*Sunday Vision* 28 March 2010). It was never accounted for. Salim Saleh is a general in the UPDF.

83   Jim Muhwezi is a lawyer and bush war veteran. He was the first Director General of the Internal Security Organisation (ISO) and a member of the Constituent Assembly that drew up the 1995 Ugandan Constitution. He served as Minister of State for Primary Education and in 1998 was censured by the

forged and taken to the Electoral Commission to get me disqualified. Since I had neither time nor money to pursue a court process, I and my supporters decided to throw all our support behind the Ndama teacher. The night before nomination, the teacher was kidnapped by state operatives and taken to Kabale. He was released after the nominations, so Muhwezi's assistant won unopposed. Shortly after that I graduated from Makerere University and had a big party here in Rukungiri. Many opposition leaders attended the function, and one of the main topics for debate was the proposed lifting of the presidential term limits. After that I was placed under surveillance by the security people.

In September 2004 I went back to Makerere for a master's course in leadership and human relations studies. Four months later, on 14 December 2004, I was arrested from my room in Dag Hammarskjöld Hall. People that I later learnt were from CMI came to my room and deceived me that they were from the police. They were led to me by Lt. Elias from Bushenyi. They said I was needed for questioning at Makerere Police Post. When I insisted that I inform the hall warden of my arrest and that I call my brother to let him know, they assured me that it was not really an arrest; I was just being taken for questioning. The warden was nonetheless informed, and he was there when we drove off. They had someone in police uniform that initially got into the car as well to reassure me, but once I got in he got out and the car sped off. I was driven to Nile Hotel and escorted to a room on the first floor,

---

Ugandan Parliament for abuse of office. He was then reappointed as a full Cabinet Minister, this time in Health. In June 2006, a Commission of Inquiry set up by the government to inquire into the misuse of the Global Fund for AIDS, Malaria, and Tuberculosis found that Jim Muhwezi and his two Ministers of State, Captain Mike Mukula and Dr. Alex Kamugisha, were responsible for misuse of public funds. He was prosecuted, and the case is still pending in Ugandan courts.

where I was told that I was under arrest for treason. The two people I remember finding in that room were Capt. Joseph Kamusiime and Lt. Enock Musinguzi. At the time a treason charge sounded so outlandish, I laughed. They informed me that George Owakukiroru and Peter, his brother, had just been arrested. I was held there till nightfall, by which time Owakukiroru and Peter were brought in. We were then transferred under heavy military escort to a house in Kololo. We were held there for six days, during which time we were beaten severely and regularly. Other treatment we were subjected to included being hit over the testicles, being made to sit on a hot plate to try and extract confessions, being threatened with snakes, and being constantly threatened with death. We were often told that if we died, nobody would know where we were. I recall a CMI soldier called Kamugisha brought a piece of paper on which was written my name, and underneath it was added, 'caught in subversive activities'. He wanted to hold it against me and to then take a picture that would incriminate me as having confessed to being involved in subversion. When I attempted to tear it up, Kamugisha hit me very hard, aiming at my testicles. I fell to the floor and blacked out. I learnt later that all this was going on within earshot of the Danish Ambassador's residence next door. There were also many other documents that we found prepared, and we were being asked to sign them.

Tweyambe recalled that the university administration did not notify the government that a student had been abducted from the campus, in the presence of the hall of residence custodian and the warden. He said it was only much later when Students' Guild President Gerald Karuhanga organized a demonstration to bring attention to his plight. He described to me how he finally entered the legal prison system.

On 19 December Peter and I were taken to CID

Headquarters. The CID officers there did not allow us to speak for ourselves; they merely took the prepared statements from CMI and asked us to sign them. We at first refused to sign, at which point we were beaten severely again to try and persuade us to sign. When I was on the verge of fainting again, a certain man from CMI took pity on us. He came and whispered to us, 'You go ahead and sign. These documents you sign here will not count in court, because there you will be allowed to tell your own story. You sign so that you can survive this stage.' So we caved in and signed those papers. At that point we had no way of knowing whether anyone out there knew of our whereabouts, whether there was any search out for us, or whether we would actually be produced in court. We had no idea at all what was happening on the outside. George had been taken from the Kololo house the morning after we were taken there, and we had been told that he was killed. We could only imagine that a similar fate awaited us. So we were in some way relieved when we were taken to Central Police Station because at least this was in view of other people, and we knew at that point that we were not going to merely disappear. But we could see that a number of the officers who were going around as police were in fact from the CMI. We were not allowed to talk to lawyers; we were not even allowed to contact our relatives.[84]

Tweyambe and Peter Atwongyeirwe were then taken to court and charged with treason and concealment of treason. They were sent to Kigo prison on remand. It was here that they met Saasi and Frank Atukunda. The group was later charged jointly with unlawful possession of firearms. They were said to belong to a rebel group, the People's Redemption Army (PRA).[85]

---

84   Interview with Darius Tweyambe, April 2009
85   The PRA was said by the government to have recruited people to fight as rebels against the government. Initially twenty-two men were jointly charged.

Courtesy the *Monitor*
Saasi, first right, together with other PRA suspects on a truck at the Military
Court Martial in Makindye.

On 16 November 2005, High Court Justice Ssempa Lugayizi granted Saasi and the other PRA suspects bail. Even before they were done signing the bail papers, the court was stormed by a new breed of security operatives, the Black Mamba Urban Hit Squad. The Black Mambas, wielding Uzi machine guns and AK-47 assault rifles, surrounded the court premises and attempted to force their way into the court's holding cells to pull out the suspects. The roads around the court premises were sealed off. In the circumstances, the prisoners preferred to go back to custody in Luzira rather than

---

When Besigye returned to Uganda, he was added to their number. I do not know if the rebel group existed and whether these twenty-two men knew each other as members of the rebel group before their meeting in prison. The treason case against those that did not accept amnesty is still in the courts.

fall into the hands of the military, whose intentions were clearly to rearrest them and take them to some unknown destination. Two days later the prisoners, who were now technically out on bail, were taken from Luzira, herded before the General Court Martial in Makindye, and charged with treason and illegal possession of firearms.

On 11 January 2007, the Constitutional Court repeated its earlier ruling on the illegality of the court martial proceedings and ordered the release of the PRA accused. When the accused were still not released, the High Court ordered that they be produced before it. The prison's authorities continued to refuse the request, prompting the High Court to summon the Commissioner General of Prisons to explain his continued reluctance to release the suspects.

One often wondered if the twenty-two men – or those that remained in jail as time went on – were as big a security threat as they were being made out to be. The full might of the military was usually on display each time they came out of their maximum security prison cells. A couple of police officers with whistles and canes would probably have been sufficient to safely bring the handcuffed men to court without the grand performances of all three armed forces, in addition to the side shows orchestrated by a host of other security outfits whose legality was in question.

In February 2007 I flew home from Harare to see Saasi, who was still in Luzira prison. He was not expecting me, so it was a truly delightful surprise. Luzira Maximum Security Prison is located on a hill overlooking a bay on Lake Victoria. The drive from central Kampala to Luzira takes one through Bugolobi, a suburb that has within it a busy and rather crowded shopping centre, a housing estate with modern apartments, and luxury homes higher up on the hill. The road running through the shopping centre takes one to Kitintale, a somewhat smaller and less wealthy suburb, with the usual mix of shops, hair dressers, car washing bays, and gas stations. In the evening the roadside becomes one long market with vendors offering all sorts of cooked food and other goods. A bit further along is the Luzira trading centre, which is even more chaotic than Kitintale, with a fresh produce market that never seems to close and whose goods are half pouring into the road. A timber yard does brisk business in the midst of a line of shops, and the *matatus* (minibus commuters) and *boda bodas* (motorcycle taxis) complete the mix.

A few meters beyond this buzz is the rather inconspicuous road that takes one to the maximum-security prison. Just out of sight from the main road is an imposing gate where prisons officers interview those wishing to visit the inmates. Once they establish that the said person is indeed incarcerated here, the officers meticulously record your personal details and relieve you of all prohibited items – money, telephone, camera, all electronic equipment. If they allow you to drive in, the vehicle is searched most carefully to ensure that nothing undesirable sneaks in. You then drive up the narrow, winding road past dilapidated staff houses, higher and higher, until the prison building comes into view. As you come closer the hill plateaus, and the road ends in a rough murram patch that serves as the parking lot. You do not take the time to look over the bay at the spectacular views offered by the prison's location because there are more prison officers waiting with more forms. You hand over your identity card. You leave whatever gifts you might have brought with you in the care of the guards, and one by one you get invited to enter the prison. The gate looks like it would withstand a tornado. The bolt is moved back, the door is swung open, and you are motioned to step inside. As soon as you step past the threshold, the door is closed behind you, and a loud metallic clang signals the bolt sliding back into place. You are inside Luzira Maximum Security Prison. It is understood that the men and women locked up here are considered dangerous to society. There are more guards milling around. You are now subjected to a body search. The ladies are given special consideration and searched by a lady officer. The prisoner is notified that a visitor is here to see him. With the final search out of the way, you are pointed to the meeting area. It is not a room. It is a solid wall up to about a meter and a half above ground, and then there are layers of thick wire mesh with space between the visitor side and the inmate side. You cannot touch the person you wish to visit. Visitor and visited can both touch the mesh and pretend that you have touched hands. All around you are people visiting in the same manner. Some have kids – they are lifting the kids high so their relatives can see them through the mesh. Everyone is talking, and everyone can listen in on other people's conversations. It is a strange way to visit.

The prison's officers let us use their office rather than reunite and talk across the wire mesh.[86] Saasi was his usual cheerful self. He came into the room with a hearty laugh and joked about everything, including the conditions in the prison. He recounted the many visits he and his colleagues had received from state operatives to try and persuade them to apply for amnesty. He said he always told them he would rather die in prison than sign the amnesty papers, in effect condemning himself for crimes he did not commit. I would later recall this conversation and realize that his had not been idle bravado – he must have known that this was a matter of life and death, and he had considered the cost during the countless nights in the dark.

But the operatives' efforts were not in vain – one by one some of the men started accepting the amnesty offer. Key among these was Owakukiroru, who the others had looked to as a leader. The blow was all the more painful to these who still maintained their innocence, because as part of the deal with the state, the amnesty group were said to have agreed to testify against their comrades. Talking to Saasi, and later to one of his friends, I could tell that they had taken the apparent betrayal pretty badly. But rather than weaken them, it seemed to have solidified their resolve – whatever happened, they were not going to bargain for their lives, even if they should die defending their innocence.

---

86   I am not sure why the officers extended this courtesy, but I remain eternally grateful. But for this opportunity I would never have been able to see my brother properly the whole time he was in jail, most of which time he was in good health. I recall seeing, much later, a highly publicized visit to Luzira by President Museveni's daughters to see their cousin Alice Kaboyo, who was held there for a couple of days. The Commission of Inquiry into the theft of Global Fund money had revealed that she had forged signatures and stashed hundreds of millions of public money onto her personal account. The prison's staff provided them a room in which to share a meal and pray.

Chapter 14: The Law of the Ruler

'A leader must do in private what he states in public. Two-faced leadership is abhorrent to me.' – Yoweri Museveni[87]

If there had been instances when the state, still purporting to champion the rule of law, broke the law with impunity, the trial of the PRA suspects brought those contradictions into sharp focus. The judiciary was caught perched uncomfortably between its high calling to uphold the constitution and ensure the administration of justice, and its continuing attempts to function normally in an increasingly abnormal environment, where the Executive expected it to do its biding.

The state had continued to hold the bailed suspects in illegal detention since November 2005. On 31 January 2007 the state, represented by the Solicitor General, applied to the High Court seeking an order to set aside the High Court bail of 16 November 2005. The Honourable Mr. Justice Mwangusya, before whom the application was brought, adjourned the application to 1 March 2007. But what was to happen to the suspects in the meantime? Were they on bail, or were they not? Seeking a way out of this illegality, which was occasioned not by the judiciary but by the executive, Justice Mwangusya remanded the bailed suspects until the date of the hearing. The suspects' lawyers learnt of this development with alarm. Almost at the point of despair, they wrote to the Principal Judge thus:

> We are writing this letter as officers of the High Court of the Republic of Uganda, enjoined to promote the proper administration of justice, and as citizens of this fair Republic, in the exercise of our constitutional right and duty to defend the Constitution…

87   Yoweri Kaguta Museveni, 'Fighting Obote', *Sowing the Mustard Seed* (London & Basingstoke: Macmillan Publishers Ltd, 1997).

The Application and the order of the [Honourable] Mr. Justice Mwangusya are grossly irregular and, if left uncorrected, will leave an indelible stain on the reputation of the Judiciary and ensure that this case continues to cast a long and ominous shadow on constitutionalism and the rule of law in this country. In our view the following questions clearly illustrate the irregularity of the Application and said order:...

In light of the declaration of the Constitutional Court... to the effect that the continuation of the trial of the Accused for treason and concealment of treason whilst the Bailed Accused are still in unlawful custody contravenes Articles 28(1), 28(3), 44(c) and 128 of the Constitution, how can the commencement and hearing of the Application against the Bailed Accused, whilst the Bailed Accused are still in unlawful custody be constitutional?

The lawyers ended their plea by asking 'that your Lordship takes the earliest opportunity to use your Lordship's good and great office to bring a swift halt to this continuing travesty of justice and affront to the Constitution of the Republic of Uganda. The citizens of the Republic of Uganda are watching the Judiciary closely'.

A month later the watchful citizens of Uganda would see how the state planned to deal with this situation.

On 1 March 2007 the PRA suspects, as they had come to be known, were brought back to court. They had been in illegal custody since 16 November 2005, when they were granted bail but were prevented from appropriating it by the invasion of the court by the Black Mambas. Between the two dates, some of the suspects had been coerced into accepting amnesty. The rest of the men now seemed set to get their bail reconfirmed. Then court siege number two commenced.

'The saga started at 11.00 AM and ended at around 8.00 PM,' recalled Mpanga.

They [security operatives] came in, sealed off the court premises where the suspects were and they tried to arrest them from the registry. At one point they made a grab for one of the suspects as he went to the toilet. He was snatched back by some vigilant spectators. They [bailed men] were stuck there. The sureties were coming in and signing the papers, but the suspects could not leave because it was clear that the security operatives would re-arrest them. This went on all day. There were many well-wishers on the premises, the press, and there were periodic contacts with the diplomatic corps. We were shuttling back and forth between the registry and the Deputy Chief Justice's office, trying to defuse the situation. We asked Grace Turyagumanawe [Regional Police Commander, Kampala] to show us a warrant of arrest, and to tell us which court they were being taken to, but there was no warrant. At one point there was an agreement with the Deputy Chief Justice that people should vacate court premises. The police asked people to leave, and eventually the premises were vacated. But the police were playing for time, probably till they would have the benefit of the cover of darkness. It was during this time when Kiyemba Mutale was telling people to leave the area that he was assaulted [by the police] and he sustained a cut on the head. [Mutale was a member of the legal defence team.] The standoff remained. Then in the evening a different group of security personnel came, walking in single file, and they entered the registry. Eventually it got pretty dark. Then the power in the entire building was switched off – everywhere it was dark except for the place where we were – at the entrance of the courtyard. The Principal Judge came out to engender confidence in the process – he announced that the bailed men were going to be taken out and released to their sureties. That is when the actual attack started. The security men grabbed the suspects and beat them severely as they bundled them onto pickup trucks. Then the trucks drove off – [we later learnt] to Bushenyi and Arua.

> It was about one man saying, 'No court is going to
> tell me what to do.'[88]

Indeed, nobody was able to stop the state from dealing with the prisoners as it pleased. While Ugandans went to bed following a

---

88   Interview with David Mpanga, December 2009.

second violent assault on its judicial system in as many years, some personnel in the security organs had a busy night. Frank Atukunda, one of the men at the centre of the court siege drama, recounted what happened.

> After waiting all day to see if we would finally be allowed to go out on bail, the soldiers pounced on us as we left the registry, beat us severely and bundled us onto pick-ups. First they took us to the Central Police Station, and then at around 4.00 AM they transferred us to CMI [on Yusuf Lule Road]. That same night our colleagues, who had not been given bail and who had in fact not had any reason to come to court that day, were somehow taken out of Luzira [prison] in the dead of night, and they were also brought to CMI. All of us were then piled into one room to await our fate. None of us slept. We hardly spoke.

> It turned out to be a relatively short wait because around nine o'clock a CMI officer came to the door, read out three names – Saasi, Darius, and I – and told us to step outside.[89] By then we should have been prepared for anything, but it was nonetheless terrifying to see the level of security on display – the parking lot was full of vehicles, with soldiers of all shades standing at the ready. Saasi was led to a military pick-up truck on his own, while Darius and I were put in a police truck. Initially Saasi was going to be put at the back of the truck, but after some heated discussion amongst the soldiers he was sat in the cabin between two heavily armed soldiers. A separate vehicle led the way; the two with us on board came next, another two vehicles, equally armed as for battle, brought up the rear. We still had no clue whatsoever where we were headed, although it

89   The other men (James Kabaka Tabuga, Yahya Amir Asiga, Idd Ahmed Yunus, Arike John, Patrick Okiring, Bruhan Dratre and Agupio Samson) were also called out shortly after and taken aboard a military helicopter to an Arua (northern Uganda) court to be charged with murder.

became clear soon enough that we were leaving the city. When we got onto Masaka road, we thought we might be destined for Mbarara barracks. After an hour or so on the road, one of the soldiers spoke up. 'How come you are so quiet?' he asked.

'We are recovering from last night's beatings,' Darius replied. Having broken the silence thus, we felt emboldened to pry for some information. 'So where are you taking us now?'

'We have instructions to deliver you to Bushenyi court. You will be charged today.'

'Charged with what offence?'

'I don't know. The charge sheet is being delivered by an officer in the vehicle behind us.'

So it was that a few hours later the five-vehicle motorcade arrived in Bushenyi. Imagine our surprise when we found a huge crowd of well-wishers thronging the town! We had been worried that nobody knew where we were being taken. True to the plan, we were taken to court and charged with murder! It was such an incredible charge that though it should have been chilling just to hear it pronounced, we actually laughed. We had been in prison for over two years on treason charges and had twice been granted bail and twice been forcefully prevented from appropriating the bail. It was an anticlimax to now hear the state come up with this latest charge. Whether the identity or existence of the alleged murder victim was complete fiction, we did not know. It would still serve the state's objective of keeping us in custody. From court we were taken to Nyamushekyera prison.

Chapter 15: The System, the System

'Without democracy and the human dignity of the African people, Africa will never develop.... The people are too frightened to comment on the actions of the omnipotent rulers that have got the powers of life and death over every citizen of their countries. Rulers can squander resources with impunity; they can violate human rights of people with impunity. Democracy, therefore, becomes a sine qua non of development. We ought to oppose dictatorship in Africa.' – Yoweri Museveni[90]

Reports of Saasi's failing health started to come out in the press in late March 2007. He missed a court appearance for the treason case, it was reported, due to illness. By this time I had left Congo and was living in Harare, Zimbabwe, where eighty-two-year-old Robert Mugabe was in his twenty-eighth year of rule. When I called home, I was told that Saasi was unwell but that it was nothing serious. Some weeks later it was again reported that he was quite ill, although the prisons authorities did not allow him to see a doctor. A couple of court hearings were missed because the state attempted to hold the sessions within the prison, but the prisoners refused to be tried under these conditions, away from public view. Each time these sessions were scheduled, there was a crowd of relatives and well-wishers outside the prison, and each time the hearing had to be abandoned because the prisoners did not show up, refusing to be tried in an ungazetted venue.

In April 2007 a group of politicians, led by Dr. Kizza Besigye and Hon. Betty Anywar, were finally allowed to enter the prison. They found the prisoners in truly deplorable conditions. Because reporters

---

90   Yoweri Museveni, *Selected Articles on the Uganda Resistance War*, 1985.

were denied entry into the cells, the world had to depend on the sordid descriptions of the politicians, which the prison authorities insisted were exaggerated to evoke public sympathy. Three years after leaving Nyamushekyera prison, Frank Atukunda and Darius Tweyambe still got the shivers when talking of their experiences there.

'The prison wards were built to accommodate forty inmates each,' Frank said.

> During our time there we were 163 men, with hardly any space between one inmate and the next. The wards are long rooms with no partitions. On one end is some space that passes for a bathroom and toilet. The flush toilets had no water; it did not seem as though there had been any water in the recent past. The waste would be piled high by afternoon, and it was emptied only once a day. There were no showers – if one found water, they would stand in the shallow trough near the toilet, scoop the precious water with hands very carefully over the head and shoulders to avoid waste, and after the 'shower' the dirty water trapped in the trough would be painstakingly retrieved by scooping it again into a bucket. This was then used to 'clean' the floor. Of course there was nothing clean in the entire place – not the floor, not the beddings, not the men – but this bath process was better than nothing. All the inmates had scabies. The doors were opened each morning around 11.00 AM when the prison staff brought the porridge to serve it in the stench accumulated from the previous day. After that we would be let out for thirty minutes and then herded back in for the rest of the day. When we had been there for a week, the three of us refused to go back in after the thirty minutes. We managed to negotiate that we be allowed to stay outside for much longer, on condition that we sat outside the warden's office in full view of the staff.

Towards the end of the first week, Saasi started to

fall sick. From having been very strong and physically fit, he started to get weak and feverish. In Luzira he always worked out in the morning, sometimes running several times around the quadrangle, and he played football almost every evening. He was never ill. But once he was taken ill, he progressed fairly quickly. We were denied permission to go to the hospital, and our pleas to have a doctor brought to the prison fell on deaf ears. We were told that there were orders from above to the effect that we were not to leave the prison under any circumstances. The only person with any medical training in the prison was a nurse aide. So Saasi was left to lie there in that stench day after day with no care whatsoever. Darius and I were his attendants, and we knew nothing about caring for a sick man with no diagnosis and no medicine. But some of the officials in the prison were very kind. One man in particular would do our shopping for foodstuffs.

In the meantime the state continued to treat us like dangerous terrorists. They installed three road blocks between the road and the prison gate, a distance of less that one kilometre. They found it necessary to supplement the police force in Bushenyi with forty more police officers from Mbarara. A guardhouse was built on the road to the prison adjacent to one of the road blocks. Initially no relatives were allowed to visit us. But a lot of those officers were very friendly and kind. They treated us with courtesy at all times. At first we were very worried, but we learnt to relax. We kept up our humour even when we were treated like terrorists. We had no trouble with the guards. We always assured them that we had no intention of escaping – and we meant it.[91]

In early May, in a sudden turn of events, the prisoners were transported

---

91   Interview with Frank Atukunda, March 2009.

back to Luzira prison to enable them attend a court hearing for the treason case. This was a big relief because the conditions in Luzira were so much better – adequate space, reasonable toilet and bath facilities, water, and the privilege of cooking their own food. But the transfer found Saasi much weakened, and it would appear he never quite recovered from the horrors of Nyamushekyera. In Luzira he continued to request for permission to see a doctor, and it was repeatedly denied. On one occasion he was told by Dr. Kakoraki that he was making up symptoms to evoke sympathy and justify his bail application. It was only after a medical assistant noticed that he had a persistently high fever, was rapidly losing weight, and hardly ate or left his room that they agreed to send him to hospital. Saasi later told me that on that day, he told the medical assistant that he felt his life was slipping away and that if he did not get treatment, he would not make it out of the prison. A nurse came and told him to get ready to be taken to hospital the next morning. That night he lay awake as he had for several nights, sweating what seemed like bucketfuls, praying that he would make it through the night. True to her word, the next morning the nurse was there to usher them to the bus. Saasi needed assistance to get onto the bus, and when they arrived at the hospital, he needed a wheelchair to take him the short distance from the bus to the doctors' consultation rooms in the casualty department. The prisons officers who took him to hospital had strict instructions to return him to prison the same day – he was not to be admitted. The doctors were horrified at his condition and immediately ordered for his admission – which created no small stir in the hospital, as the prisons authorities had not planned on this turn of events. After a flurry of frantic phone calls, some of which sought to reverse the admission order, they eventually settled for accommodation on the top floor of the hospital, where it would be easier to keep him under constant armed surveillance and in a room from which he could not possibly escape. Never mind that he was practically bedridden, unable to make the few short steps to the bathroom.

The weeks that followed would see him guarded by armed prison officers, as well as a host of other military and paramilitary agents. They followed him everywhere – to the X-ray department, the heart institute, the laboratory; they were a constant irritant to everyone, including the medical personnel. At least one of the guards was constantly in the room wielding a loaded gun, while a few more lounged outside his room interrogating visitors. Initially they were present during even the most intimate medical examinations until the doctors insisted that he be allowed privacy like other patients. But he was not allowed to receive visitors without the ever-present guards, and he had no access to the phone.

One day in April 2007, I received a phone call from Besigye. He told me that all attempts to get Saasi bail had failed because the lawyers needed some medical report that nobody seemed willing or able to provide. I knew that Besigye must have tried everything – just how difficult could it be to get a medical report on a hospitalized patient? I was soon to find out.

The day after I talked to Besigye, I flew home from Harare to see Saasi, in the belief that if all that was necessary to apply for bail was a medical report, I would have it in a few hours of showing up at the hospital. I had worked for several years as a surgeon at this same hospital; I knew pretty much everyone from the director to the cleaners, and I had always found most of these people to be hard working and highly principled. When I arrived Besigye told me that the substantive director was away and that the acting director, at the time Mr. Sam Mutumba, had told him he could not provide a medical report. My first stop was the director's office. I found my friend and former boss Mr. Isaac Ezati, who was the deputy director. He knew why I was there, and he expressed sympathy for my brother's condition. After a few pleasantries I explained that my brother's condition was indeed grave and that the only technicality that stood between him and bail was the lack of a medical report, which he could so easily provide. At the mention of the report, Isaac's demeanour changed. He looked very uncomfortable. He explained to me, ever so apologetically, that he really could not provide this report, or even make the specialists looking after Saasi to provide one.

'Why not,' I asked.

'Well, you see, your brother's case is very, *very* sensitive. It is very political. We cannot simply write a report.'

'But surely, every patient has a right to information about their condition. We are not asking that the doctors say anything that is not true. The doctors need not concern themselves with the politics. All Saasi needs is a factual statement of his state of health. Is he not entitled to this?' I insisted.

'No, it is not that simple. You see, your brother is really not our patient.'

I bit my lip to stop myself blurting out something that would be unhelpful to my cause. Isaac continued. 'Your brother is under the care of the Prisons Department in the Ministry of Internal Affairs. If they want a report, they will ask us to provide one; then we can provide it. In fact even if such a report were made, it would not be given to the patient or his relatives. It would go directly and confidentially to the Commissioner of Prisons, who would be at liberty to do with it as he pleases. So far the Prisons Department has not asked us for a report.'

I realized that nothing I said would persuade Isaac to change his position. At a certain level I felt sorry for him. I felt sorry for them all. What did they fear? What could possibility happen to the doctor who chose to do what they believed to be in the patient's best interest, even if that might not be at the state's pleasure? I tried a different approach.

'So who do I talk to? The Commissioner for Prisons? Saasi's lawyers have told me that they already made the rounds, and they were told the hospital needs to provide the report.' Isaac was relieved to get me off his case and advised me to speak to Dr. Nyabwana, the Director of Medical Services for the Prisons.

I left Isaac's office and stopped at the secretary's desk to get Dr. Nyabwana's phone number. He picked up at the second ring; I was in luck. I introduced myself briefly and asked if I could pop over to see him. He said he was not going to be in the office for very long, but I assured him I would be there very shortly. I dashed to the car and sped to Dr. Nyabwana's office. I found him talking to a gentleman that he introduced as Dr. Kakoraki. Red warning lights were going off in my head at the mention of that name, but I did not let that get in the way. After a brief chat I mentioned that I was there to sort out the small matter concerning my young brother.

'Which young brother is this?' he wanted to know.

'You will probably have heard of him. He is called Joseph Musasizi. He is right now admitted at Mulago in Ward 6A.'

If this had not been such a desperate situation, I would have had a good laugh at Dr. Nyabwana's reaction. His face changed from friendly and open to mildly curious, to reserved, and finally to near hostile. His structures were set as if to say, 'I know this is trouble, I have decided how I am going to handle it, and I will entertain no departure from my position.' But Dr. Nyabwana is a gentleman, and I suppose he got where he was by knowing how to deal with people. He was probably having a good day till I showed up, and I felt somewhat sorry that I was spoiling it. But my kid brother was lying in hospital slowly fading away, and Dr. Nyabwana worked for the same system that had denied him care. I was not about to provide him with excuses. He explained, pretty much in the same manner that Isaac had done earlier, that this was a very sensitive matter and that they had to be very careful about what they did. I again pointed out that I understood from having looked after patients myself that medical personnel were expected to uphold the highest code of conduct, to stay with the facts, and to do everything in the interest of their patients. We all seemed to be in agreement in this. I further mentioned that the patient did not want the prison's department, or the hospital, to provide any information that was untrue. All he asked was that they provide him with a report stating the condition of his health. Surely this was not too much to ask?

Dr. Nyabwana gave me the kind of look that grown-ups reserve for naïve children. 'Dr. Kobusingye,' he started, 'what you say is true, but the system does not work like that. Your brother's lawyers must know this. I suppose they have already been to court, and they have been told that if the bail is being sought on medical grounds, they need a medical report. With that statement from the court, they should write to the Commissioner General requesting for the report and giving reasons why they need this report. The Commissioner

General will then refer the matter to me, and I will in turn write to Mulago Hospital requesting that they provide us with an update on the condition of our patient.' He had thrown me a lifeline. At least he had told me what this monster of a system wanted for dinner. I grabbed it.

'Can I bring the letter to you? I am sure you will be able to direct it to the right office so that it comes to you without delay.'

Without waiting for him to answer, I pulled out my phone and right there in his office called David Mpanga, one of the lawyers. I repeated what Dr. Nyabwana had told me, all the while looking Dr. Nyabwana in the face for confirmation, and asked if Mpanga would write the letter. He said, and I repeated it loudly for Dr. Nyabwana's benefit, that it would be ready by the time I got to his office, which was a mere five minutes away. After securing Dr. Nyabwana's assurance that he would indeed follow up with the request to the hospital, I tore out of there and ran to Mpanga's chambers. The letter was delivered, and the request was sent to the hospital. However, straightforward as the whole process sounded, no report had been made three days later when my time was over and I had to go back to Harare. In fact the letter did not get delivered for another ten days after it was requested.

Besigye told me he had been through this sort of obstruction count-less times, over everything – asking for bail, asking to have his passport when he needed to travel (a few times the key person in the process disappeared and conveniently showed up the day after Besigye should have travelled), securing court appearances… it was easy to understand how he became so worn out, simply taking care of the basics. But this was not just a court appearance, not a trip to attend a meeting – it was trying to get his young brother out of the clutches of the state no matter how temporarily, and it was proving impossible.

While the lawyers, the prison authorities, and the judiciary played ping pong with the bail process, the doctors spared no effort in trying to get Saasi back on his feet. Initially the state flatly refused Saasi's family to participate in his care. All prescriptions had to be taken to a series of offices back in the Prisons Department in order for money to be released for the medicine purchases. This led to frustrating delays in starting medication.

A few weeks later, after many more trying encounters with the system, Saasi's bail was finally secured. The man who had just a day earlier been heavily guarded by gun-wielding military personnel would now be allowed to move up and down the extensive hospital grounds without so much as a security guard glancing his way. Saasi had been in illegal detention for one year and seven months. We were all thankful for this relative freedom, though the day he was actually allowed home there was plenty of anxiety about his safety. Much of that anxiety was in our minds – Saasi himself was elated to go to his house and to hang out with his wife and kids, and he was going to do it even if we all thought his house would be a target. The night before he was formally discharged, he went home to have dinner with the family, and the event rapidly turned into a thunderous homecoming party. Friends and family who heard that he was home all congregated at his house, and some called friends and family several flying hours away so they too could share in the excitement of the moment.

On further reflection, the behaviour of the doctors was not a rare phenomenon. History is replete with stories of doctors and other health care professionals who were torn between their professional obligation and desire to care for sick people, and a regime's determination to harm individuals opposed to it by denying them health care. One of the better known cases in Africa is that of Steven Biko, the South African freedom activist perhaps best remembered for Black Consciousness, and his pursuit for nonviolent change. Like Mamenero, Steve Biko was assaulted by security operatives; he sustained a severe head injury and died of his injury while in custody. But unlike Mamenero, Biko was actually examined by doctors who declared that he was well, even though he had visible injuries and was almost comatose. When he died on a cold stone floor a day later, still shackled on the legs, the Minister in charge of the police declared that he had died as a result of a hunger strike.

In November 2007 Saasi was taken ill again. He called and told me he was being treated for malaria. By the third day he was so ill that he was moved to the intensive care unit. The day before he died, I was on the phone with Kampala numerous times. I talked to Besigye, the doctors, Saasi's wife, and then I repeated the rounds, occasionally drawing in new medical specialists at Besigye's suggestion. He seemed to have become a permanent fixture in the intensive care unit at Mulago Hospital. At night we discussed the possibility of moving him to Nairobi, where he could get better care. Besigye did not disagree, but he sounded doubtful about the feasibility of moving Saasi given the severity of his condition. He also reminded me that Saasi had no passport (it expired while he was in prison) and that their application to allow him get a new one was still lying somewhere in the cavernous and obtrusive court system. I went to bed with several scenarios going through my mind, all rotating around the safest way to move him to better care.

In the morning I had a teleconference and was taking the call in a colleague's office across the corridor from mine. During the teleconference I got a phone call from Besigye to say that Saasi had taken a turn for the worse and was now very restless. I went to my office and called one of the doctors to get a more detailed update. He confirmed what Besigye had said but also assured me that they were working hard to stabilize him. They were sending Besigye to the pharmacy to buy some more medication. I went back to the teleconference but cannot recall one word that was said after that call with Kampala. A few minutes after the conference ended, a call from an unknown number came through on my cell phone – as soon as I answered it, the person at the other end started to wail. I shut it off and sat frozen in my chair, my heart thumping loudly and my head spinning. After a few minutes I gathered the courage to call my sister-in-law, Christine. I do not recall if I asked her anything, or if she just blurted it out on hearing my voice: yes, Saasi had just passed away, a few minutes before Besigye returned with the medicine.

I could just picture him walking in, with his measured long strides and forehead creased and shoulders slightly hunched, clutching a paper bag with the medicine which would now never be needed. I could imagine him stopping a few steps short of the bed, taking in the positions and expressions of the doctors, who were probably by this time removing the intravenous lines and drawing the sheet over his young brother's silent and still face. I could imagine him but could not begin to imagine what thoughts must have gone through his head. Standing there, exhausted, alone, alive, watching as his young brother, who had been so alive and full of plans only a few days ago, was now deceased. I could picture him walking out again, past the pile of shoes at the entrance of the intensive care unit, where all shoes must be removed and replaced with the white clogs if one is allowed to enter. In my mind's eye I could see him walking past the nurses in their green scrub uniforms. He would be contemplating what lay ahead – the relatives waiting outside, the crowds of people that would soon be gathering at the house, the press, the meetings to plan his kid brother's funeral.… It always seemed that he was constantly surrounded by people, but he was in some odd inexplicable way always alone – the costly icon of resistance. Anyone who wanted to know what it was like to oppose Museveni need never wonder. And having a young brother die in this manner seemed so much a part of that wretched role. But even while I tottered on the verge of disintegration, I counted myself fortunate that I could just take a plane and go home. My exiled sister Margaret did not have that luxury.

The day after Saasi died, I got home to find precisely the kind of scenes that I had wished to avoid. While I had expected a fair amount of press coverage of the death, what I had not expected were statements from the political opposition, accompanied by vehement denials by the government, that Saasi's death was the result of foul play by the state. 'I reject the allegations because they are false. He was sick and treated while he was in prison. People should be responsible with statements that they make and have evidence for whatever they say,' said Dr. Ruhakana Rugunda, Minister of Internal Affairs. I did not know if Dr. Rugunda ever visited prisons like Nyamushekyera. I did not know if he ever got reports from the doctors employed by the Prisons Department. What I did know was that Saasi had been transferred from Luzira Prison to Mulago Hospital unable to walk, hardly able to eat, and with most of his body systems near collapse. He had been in detention continuously for two and a half years prior to that hospital admission. I had seen Saasi a few months before in prison, and as far as I could tell he had been in perfect health. If the prison's doctors had treated Saasi, Dr. Rugunda had to choose whether his doctors were so incompetent that they had not noticed that one of their prisoners was close to death, or so criminally negligent that they saw it but did nothing about it.

Ironically, the possibility of people being killed by poisoning or the introduction of harmful infectious agents while in Ugandan prisons or hospitals had been advanced by President Museveni. In 2003 the presidential jet was used to fly Natasha Karugire, Museveni's daughter, to a German hospital to have a baby. The first family was heavily criticized for their lavish lifestyle at the expense of impoverished tax payers. Many pointed out that Natasha could have had the best obstetric care in all of Uganda but that she had chosen to have her baby in a German hospital at a huge cost, at a time when the majority of Ugandan babies were being delivered without any medical care whatsoever. Museveni was quick to point out how much Ugandans stood to benefit from his family seeking medical care in foreign capitals.

> I need to enlighten Ugandans about the need for my family or myself getting check-up or treatment abroad at all…. The fact that I do not only detest but also hold in deep contempt a wasteful life-style is well known to Ugandans except those blinded by greed and envy. However, when it comes to security of myself, my family and my country there is no (and there will never be) any compromise. It is now almost 40 years that I have been fighting for the emancipation of Uganda, mainly, and, to a reasonable extent, for Africa. As head of the Resistance Movement for most of this time, I resolved never to donate myself to the criminal killers of the African peoples – the ones that have caused so much misery for our people.

Then he elaborated on how contact with the Ugandan health care system might be hazardous.

> Defending ourselves against the enemy means doing

so against his bullets, his land-mines or bombs, his chemical agents (poisoning) or his biological agents (poisoning through introduction of bacteria or viruses into one's body).... Consequently, in spite of being in Kampala for 17 years now, I have never rushed into a clinic and had my veins pierced in order to draw my blood for examination. I do it in a certain controlled way or do it abroad. Even abroad we take precautions.

And in case all this sounded too far-fetched, almost fictitious, Museveni gave examples close to home.

There was a famous General in Nigeria who was infected with incurable biological agents by 'doctors' of the Abacha regime when they came to take his blood for examination. Another General who was in the same prison refused and he is very much alive and around. The other died a very painful death. Therefore, the question of myself and my family getting medical check-up or treatment abroad, where necessary, is unavoidable. It is part of our survival strategy in still hostile circumstances, in order to continue to fight for our country.[92]

So was it technically possible that a vulnerable prisoner or a patient in hospital could be poisoned? According to Museveni, the answer was yes. The possibility was real enough that he chose to go elsewhere when he needed to see doctors. Despite Dr. Rugunda's assurances, many people remained convinced that the state had a hand in Saasi's death. Those who did not want to contemplate the more sinister methods described by the President still pointed to Saasi's denial of health care until very late in his illness.[93]

---

92   Letter by President Museveni, printed in the *Monitor*, 5 October 2003.

93   Two years after Saasi's death, I asked one of the doctors who had looked after him why the medical team had found it so difficult to provide a medical report. Without hesitation, the doctor had one answer: fear. When I pressed him to elaborate, he said doctors had been taken out of Mulago Hospital and killed in previous regimes, and he did not want to take chances, having seen how Saasi was being treated.

In early July 2009, Besigye and his co-accused and their lawyers were back at the Constitutional Court in connection with the court siege. I had now moved back home and could attend court sessions with ease. On the appointed day, eight o'clock found me seated at the court. This was supposed to be an important event. It was to determine if the state had a case to answer the claims concerning the events of 1 March 2007, when state security operatives stormed the High Court and assaulted and abducted prisoners who had just been given bail. I thought the court room might be full. The court siege had been very public and had been condemned by the judiciary, the Uganda Law Society, and civil society. The judges had staged a sit-down strike to protest what they saw as an attempt by the state to intimidate and neuter the judiciary. Following the second court siege, the International Bar Association had dispatched a high-level delegation as part of their rapid-response mechanism to investigate the circumstances and implications of the siege for judicial independence and the rule of law.[94] The East African Court of Justice had ruled that the court siege by security agencies in November 2005 violated the rule of law and that the blocking of the suspects from accessing the bail that had been granted them contravened the East African Community Treaty.[95] The court had further ruled that action militated against the independence of the judiciary.

I was therefore somewhat surprised to find the small courtroom half empty – a couple of lawyers representing the state, lawyers for the bailed suspects, three of the men who had been abducted, and one or two other people – family or friends of the prisoners. There were four journalists in attendance. The judges came in and the proceedings started. There were a few exchanges back and forth as the facts were restated, the import of which was that the state had raided the court and assaulted bail applicants twice, first on 16 November 2005 and then again on 1 March 2007. The case now appeared only of interest to a small group of people: the men who had been assaulted, their lawyers, and some in the judiciary.

---

94   'Judicial Independence Undermined: A Report on Uganda'. International Bar Association Human Rights Institute. September 2007. http://www.ibanet.org/Human_Rights_Institute/HRI_Publications/Country_reports.aspx

95   *Sunday Vision*, 4 November 2007

I could think of many reasons why there were not more people in attendance: dates for such hearings are not well publicised; people with meagre earnings can ill afford the time for court hearings; exchanges between lawyers and judges sound like a foreign language to most people; people hold out little hope of real change coming by way of the courts. Whatever the reason, this apathy did not augur well for the cause of justice.

In late July 2009, I went to South Africa on business. Margaret was also going to be in Johannesburg for a few days, so we planned to meet and catch up. The weather was very harsh, with single-digit temperatures during the day and below freezing at night. Margaret's legendary dislike for cold weather was at its worst. She took a taxi to the suburb north of Johannesburg, where I was staying, and emerged from the car looking like she was expecting a snowstorm. We spent a lovely evening chatting about all sorts of things, mostly relatives and friends in Uganda and elsewhere. The following day she had to go back to downtown Johannesburg. She flatly refused to take a taxi, saying it was way too expensive. We could not take her all the way down because I was rushing to the airport, so my host looked for a place to drop her off so she could find public transport. When we finally located the bus stop, she got out of the car and walked to the bus all wrapped up in sweaters and scarves, despite the fact that it was a little warmer now that the sun was out. I could remember a time when she would not have taken public transport in Johannesburg in July. But this was 2009, and Margaret did not have a car, did not have a home, did not have a business to run, so she did not have a tight schedule. Was she on her way to becoming stateless? I was still having this conversation with myself when she stood at the bus entrance, looked back, and waved cheerfully before disappearing into the bus. I wondered how many other Ugandans were out there, planning to return home but never knowing how or when that might happen.

On 18 September 2009, two and a half years after the state charged Saasi and his colleagues with murder, the charges were officially dropped. Out of public view, in a small and unassuming courtroom in Bushenyi, the Magistrate stated that the Director of Public

Prosecution had decided to discontinue proceedings. Charges against the men who had been taken to Arua were similarly dropped without explanation. The state never produced a single witness; they never presented one iota of evidence. The only record in existence concerning murder charges was the charge sheets that were used to justify the men's imprisonment. It gave no details of the person who Saasi and colleagues were alleged to have murdered – no age, no address, no next-of-kin, and no previous occupation. Journalists who tried to track down the man's family or village could not locate one person who knew of such a person or such a murder. The Local Council leaders had never heard of the person or the murder, which was very surprising because they would have been informed of such a serious occurrence. Police officers in Bushenyi had confessed that they knew nothing of the case, which seemed to have had its origins in the office of the Director of Public Prosecution, and not with the police. With the case now closed, it will never be known whether indeed a murder victim ever existed.

Chapter 16: The Storyteller Is Dead

'The NRM never uses the radio or newspapers for its own causes; if anything the radio and the newspapers are used more by the opposition than by us.' – Yoweri Museveni[96]

'There is nothing that should ever justify the killing or imprisonment of a journalist for something they have either written or said. You should respond if you disagree.' Wafula Oguttu told me this in response to my question concerning where the balance lay between journalistic independence and responsibility. Oguttu was well placed to make this judgment, having been a journalist and newspaper editor for most of his working life under different regimes. I found Wafula's appearance somewhat understated for a man that worked as the chief publicist for the largest opposition party in the country. The smooth, round face and alert eyes contrasted rather sharply with the balding head, making it difficult to guess his age. The easy smile broke out into a hearty laugh. His dress was casual; he would go unnoticed in any crowd. He enjoyed recounting stories from his days as a journalist. When he talked about journalism, his face and body took on a new energy, and his responses betrayed a sharp mind that has spent a great deal of time synthesizing ideas. He expressed concern, but not surprise, at the shrinking media freedoms in the Uganda over the last several years.

> In my days as a journalist and editor, I used to keep a night bag in my office in preparation for the day I would be arrested and taken to jail over my work.

---

96   Yoweri Kaguta Museveni, 'Building a Democratic Future', *Sowing the Mustard Seed* (London & Basingstoke: Macmillan Publishers Ltd, 1997). Reprinted 'with corrections' in 2007.

And one day it happened. I was arrested over a story I wrote to the effect that Museveni had reprimanded his cabinet for being inefficient. I had mentioned the names of the Ministers that were reprimanded. Cosmas Adyebo was the Prime Minister then, and Abu Mayanja was the Attorney General. It is possible that he [Mayanja] had given the nod for me to be arrested. The Ministers knew that although the story was true, cabinet meeting minutes were confidential so I would have no evidence. The following morning there was a crowd outside the CPS to see me and to find out why I had been arrested. In the end the government 'lost interest' in the case, and I was released without charge but without apology either. Another time some soldiers were unhappy with us [the *Monitor*] over a story we had run involving the military. We were told that some in the army had wanted to harm us, but others were concerned for our safety and wanted to give us armed guards to protect us. I refused. I said I would not have armed guards, and if anybody wanted to kill me, so be it. Then in February 2002, the *Monitor* ran a story on a UPDF helicopter that had crashed while fighting Kony in northern Uganda. Museveni sent soldiers to ransack and surround the *Monitor* offices for one week. They pulled down our servers and took some computers and computer accessories, as well as some 100 box files. They seemed to be very certain what files they wanted: mainly to do with the military and the Ugandan army's involvement in the Congo. We also had files on the involvement of Kazini and Mayombo in the Congo war, the plunder that went on, and transactions with business people involved in the same trade. The *Monitor* was closed for a week after the raid.[97]

On 12 January 2002, Jimmy Higenyi, a student at a private journalism

97   Interview with Wafula Ogutu, December 2009.

school, United Media Consultants and Trainers, was shot by police while covering a rally of the opposition party Uganda People's Congress in the capital, Kampala. The government had banned the gathering, and police officers fired into the crowd, hitting Higenyi, who died instantly. Although Higenyi did not seem to have been killed because he was a journalist, that is how the story was portrayed. This was quite shocking because Uganda had the reputation of having one of the most liberalized media on the continent. I asked Oguttu about this apparent contradiction. He was quick to explain.

It is often said that Uganda has maybe the largest number of radio stations in Africa. Yes, we have about 200 radio stations, we have about 12 newspapers. But who owns them? The state-owned *New Vision* empire owns most of the papers, and now it has gone into the radio stations. They are a major owner. Close to 90 per cent of radio stations are owned by people in government – ministers, army generals, and police officers – or businessmen who are very close to the regime. If you are not pro-government, you are not given a license or a frequency. I applied for a frequency and a license to operate a radio station. This was not a personal application; I was part of a company. We paid for the license, and they even gazetted the name in the newspapers to ask if anybody had an objection. As soon as it was known that I was in [opposition] politics, the license was denied. They kept giving excuses. In the end someone told the company that they would not get a license until and unless I left the board. FDC cannot get a frequency. DP, UPC, they cannot get frequencies or licenses to operate radio stations. When the applications are received, the applicants are told that the issuing of licensing has been suspended. Today when you are setting up a radio station, the application has to include pictures of all board members and copies of their birth certificates, and so there is no way a person can hide.

John Kazoora, bush war veteran and former MP, described to me what has happened to the media as part of a wider problem.

> Museveni does not want any institution to be strong and functional. He has them in a tight stranglehold, and they have all been shredded. The first one was the army; it was made sectarian and personalized. Then came the judiciary. So now what we have, although some people do not want to acknowledge it, is a one-man's rule. There is no tolerance. What the one man says goes. The only thing that was left was the press. Now that too is gone. The recent riots gave him the perfect opportunity to crack down on the journalists.

Kazoora was referring to the September 2009 riots that broke out in Kampala and a few other towns in Buganda following the government's refusal of Kabaka (king) Mutebi to visit Kayunga, a part of the Buganda Kingdom. The government had warned that a subgroup of the Baganda in Kayunga did not want the Kabaka to visit the area without first consulting their head, and that they posed a security risk to the King.

Kazoora continued. 'I remember Museveni commenting on Kony: he said it is no longer necessary to pick up guns; instead of guns you can pick up the microphone – Museveni's own words – that people who disagree should pick up the microphone and talk, instead of picking up arms. Now journalists have been arrested and charged, radio stations are closed.'[98]

Kazoora was one of those people that joined the bush war the day they finished university. He talked of the sacrifices that he and his friends had made and of the sense of betrayal at the stolen revolution. Then with a cryptic smile spreading across his face, he turned and asked me if I knew much about foxes. Foxes? No, I admitted I knew nothing about foxes. 'The fox always cried in the night,' Kazoora started. 'But one day it started to whistle in broad daylight. This was very surprising indeed. So someone asked the fox why he was doing

---

98   Interview with John Kazoora, October 2009.

something completely out of character, to which the fox replied, "*Akeshoni kawheire!*" "The time for cover-up is over!'" At this Kazoora threw his head back and laughed. 'Museveni has come to that point: the time for cover-up is over.'

Robert Kalundi Serumaga, one of the journalists who had been abducted and held in illegal detention following a television broadcast, was reluctant to be drawn into conversation about his ordeal. He said the writing should have been on the wall the day Museveni declared at a press conference in 1987, 'I am putting journalists on notice that if they malign the good name of the NRA, they will be locked up under the detention laws.' According to Serumaga, the implication was that Museveni would use the dreaded laws left on the books by Obote's dictatorial regime. Indeed, over the years but increasingly since 2000, journalists have been arrested and charged with sedition and defamation; radio stations have been threatened with closure, and some have been closed. On 22 June 2003, Kyoga Veritus radio, which was run by the Catholic Church, was raided by the police. They shut it down and carried away all their equipment. The government did not like the radio reporting on the insurgency in the north. It took the intervention of Parliament to get it reopened weeks later. In September 2009 four radio stations were closed following the riots that rocked Kampala in relation to a stand-off between the government and the Buganda Kingdom. They were accused of inciting violence.

The state has been instrumental in denying opposition politicians, especially Besigye, access to radio, particularly in up-country stations. In one incident it was reported that the Resident District Commissioner in Kitgum, Nahaman Ojwee, forcefully switched Kitti FM radio station's power generator off thirty minutes into a two-hour live programme because the management had accepted to host Besigye on the talk show. The radio remained off air for several hours. The managers of the station were later questioned by the police.[99] On 3 February 2010, Luo FM in the Pader district cancelled a radio broadcast on which Besigye was going to speak. The time slot had been paid for, but the station managers cited orders from above

---

99   *Monitor*, 31 May 2007.

as they refunded the money.[100] The 'orders from above' were popping up in many places. It seems that for the media, the time for cover-up ended a long time ago.

---

100   *Monitor,* 5 February 2010.

Chapter 17: No Mystery about the Gun: It Kills People

'In the past armies belonged to individuals and not to Uganda. We believe that armies should be national and nationalist. They should not be swept away by changes of government or by the exit of individuals from power. That is why we attach the greatest importance to the politicization of our soldiers. They must assimilate the aspirations of all the citizens of Uganda so that they can learn to serve them all, and not just individuals or sections of the community.' – Yoweri Museveni [101]

The harassment and intimidation of the people, which had gone largely unchallenged in earlier elections, became widespread in the run-up to the 2001 elections. On 13 December 2000, fifty-seven-year-old John Oloka from Aswa County in Gulu was arrested while holding a meeting in support of Besigye. He was the coordinator of the Elect Kizza Besigye Task Force in the county. Before the meeting he had sought the permission of the local authorities. He later narrated his ordeal to Human Rights Watch:

> So I held a meeting attended by many people. We discussed and people elected representatives for the Besigye campaign. Before I wound up my speech I saw a man in plain dress who stood just by the door. He asked me who I was... then I showed him my agent's appointment letter which bears Dr Besigye's symbols. So he looked at it and then said, 'Okay, you are the right people I was looking for. In my area I

101   Yoweri K. Museveni, 'Was It a Fundamental Change?' *What Is Africa's Problem?* (University of Minnesota Press, 2000).

don't want to hear any other campaign agents apart from Yoweri Museveni's campaigners. Because of these matters I am going to arrest you.' I said, if you want to arrest me you can do so but I am behind the law because the law says the consultative meeting can be held in the room. The man was a lieutenant [later identified as Lt. David Kitala]. He called some other army personnel in uniform and ordered them to arrest me.

Oloka was beaten with rifles on the neck and chest in the presence of other participants of the meeting, and the soldiers took him to the nearby army detachment:

When they took me to the barracks and ordered me to lie down I was caned badly on my buttocks. Then they tied me up with a rope, just on the side of my leg, touching my testicles. After doing that, they threw me into the cells.

He said he stayed in military detention in the cell for two days and nights and did not get any food or drink, nor was he given toilet facilities. After the two days he was taken to Gulu army barracks, where an officer told him he should have sought permission from the army to hold the meeting. He was then taken to the police, where he was told he was going to be charged with trespassing. He was held there two more days before being released without charge. During the first two days of his detention, Oloka's family did not know where he was held. Only when he arrived at the police station did he manage to contact his family. Since his arrest he has had health problems:

I don't sleep. I only rest on bed, always, not asleep. Even up to now when it is quiet, I can hear a sound from my ears. Even my neck is still not yet cured. [102]

---

102   Human Rights Watch. 'Uganda: Not a Level Playing Field: Government Violations in the Lead-up to the Election', 1 February 2001. A1301, available at http://www/unhcr.org/refworld/docid/3ae6a87c0.html [accessed 11 September 2009].

The period before the nomination of presidential candidates was full of tension and suspicion as the aspiring candidates went around the country conducting consultations with the electorate. Contrary to the law, serving military officers were making threatening political statements, and many civil servants who should have remained neutral openly adopted partisan positions in support of Museveni. In response to media reports stating that 80 per cent of the army supported Besigye's candidacy, Museveni was reported to have told a rally in Western Uganda, 'How do they support him? I am the one who trained them. They listen to me because I am the president. How do they listen to him? How does he go on radio and claim such? Who is he? No army can listen to Besigye beyond the rule of President Museveni.'

At this time, the army and the police regularly dispersed any public gatherings that did not sing Museveni's songs. On 18 December 2000, police shot at people attending a rally by Sebaggala, who was conducting consultations for his presidential bid.

On 12 January 2001, two agents of the Elect Kizza Besigye Task Force were killed in Mbale district in Eastern Uganda. According to testimonies collected by Human Rights Watch, several armed men, who turned out to be members of the Local Defence Unit, came to the house of Hussein Namonye, a campaign agent for Dr. Kizza Besigye in Mbale. When Namonye came out of the house, he mistook them for robbers and tried to apprehend one of them, but he was shot and wounded in the chest. After about twenty minutes the men came back with bricks and stoned Namonye to death. When an older son tried to raise an alarm, the attackers took him to the police station, accusing him of killing his father. On the day of his death, Namonye had been putting up posters of Besigye in Mbale. The attackers reportedly did not take anything from the house. These cases were not investigated by the police, and the offenders were never brought to trial. Elsewhere in the same district, Mohammed Kasubi, a supporter of Dr. Kizza Besigye, was seen during the day putting up posters of his candidate and was seen returning to Nakaloke. He was found unconscious the next morning, and was partly undressed. He died in Mbale hospital later that morning.

In the early hours of 4 February 2001, the day Besigye was scheduled to address a rally in Mukono, a gruesome incident occurred in Kazinga zone, Namanve, twelve kilometres along the Kampala–Jinja highway. Some Besigye supporters had come out to sweep the roads and to decorate the roadsides ahead of the rally. A double-cabin pick-up truck drove past, made a U-turn a short distance down the road, and drove back at full speed, mowing through the group of supporters as they tried to scamper to safety. It was reported that one of the occupants of the truck was in military uniform and that the vehicle belonged to Major Oula, a resident of Kireka, a Kampala suburb not too far from the scene of the crash. The police arrived at the scene shortly after the crime, and Joseph Katuramu, then Division Police Commander at Jinja Road Police Station, confirmed that three people died in the incident. Two young women and a man survived with severe multiple injuries and were admitted to Mulago Hospital. There is no record of any investigation, and nobody was ever prosecuted for the crime.

On 12 February 2001 at around 2.00 AM, Hajji Ramathan Muwonge; his son Siraje Wamala; and a visitor, Kaamu Benjamin, were arrested in Makindye by armed men who wore civilian clothes and military boots. Hajji Muwonge was a businessman and the vice chairman of the Elect Besigye Task Force in Makindye, Kampala. The assailants were armed with sticks and guns. They broke into the house, found Hajji Muwonge and his wife hiding under the bed, and proceeded to drag them out and beat them. Hajji Muwonge told Human Rights Watch:

> They [the soldiers] start holding me and just beat me too much... There were about twenty people who came to my room... I told them, 'What do you want? You want money? You want other things? You want what?' They said, 'No... You don't want our candidate Museveni... Today you are going to be killed because you don't want Museveni.'[103]

---

103   Human Rights Watch, 'Uganda: Not a Level Playing Field: Government Violations in the Lead-up to the Election', 1 February 2001. http://www.unhcr.org/cgi-bin/texis/vtx/refworld/rwmain?page=printdoc&docid=3ae6 [accessed 9 Nov 2009].

A twenty-three-year-old nurse who was also sleeping in the house reported being beaten and threatened with rape by the soldiers who attempted to undress her. According to Hajji Muwonge, he, his son, and their visitor were seized and taken outside, where the attackers discussed whether they should kill Hajji Muwonge or transport him to the place they had been directed to take him. The group was then taken to the Mbuya army barracks. Hajji Muwonge was caned the next morning, and Kaamu Benjamin was stripped naked. The following day at about 3.00 PM, they were released by Chief of Military Intelligence Lt. Col. Mayombo, who told Human Rights Watch that Muwonge should never have been arrested. He said he had initiated a disciplinary inquiry into the actions of the Mbuya barracks soldiers that night. In their defence, the soldiers claimed that Mr. Muwonge and the two other men were abducted by unknown attackers and brought to Mbuya barracks as suspects. On 1 March 2001, three soldiers were sentenced to three months in prison after pleading guilty to receiving Mr. Muwonge at Mbuya barracks 'without clear instructions from the relevant authorities'. The tribunal cited mitigating factors in sentencing them on the grounds that they were new soldiers who were unaware of the procedures.

Incidents of harassment, intimidation, and torture were in fact rampant all over the country. Various campaign teams had formed human rights desks, or desks to record and report offences related to the elections. These groups became so overwhelmed by the number of incidents that from morning till late at night the officers working at these desks were running from investigating one incident to the next and were hardly able to keep up. They were constantly registering cases at the local police stations, which seemed to have been converted into centres for reporting electoral violence and other malpractices. But the police themselves were actively engaged in perpetuating some of the offences, as in the examples above. Rhoda Mirembe of Rukungiri was arrested a total of nine times by the police in the one month before the presidential polls. On every occasion, between USh 20,000–50,000 (US$14–34) was needed to get her released on police bond. A week before the elections, PPU soldiers came to her house looking for her but found her in hiding. They destroyed her vehicle, which was parked outside her house, and did not leave one window or mirror intact. The soldiers were overheard saying they were doing to the car what they had planned to do to her. She recounted her story as follows:

> During the presidential campaign of 2001, a UPDF Lieutenant called Ndahura[104] put a pistol in my mouth. He found us at a rally in Bwambara and tried to disperse the people. The soldiers shot in the air, and many people scampered for cover. I was standing on a pick-up truck with a microphone in my hand. When I heard the gun shots, I did not jump off. I remained standing, frozen in the spot. After a short while, Ndahura walked over and told me to dismantle the public address system and go away. I told him I did not know how to take it apart. He ordered me to switch off the generator. I still remained rooted on the spot. He dragged me down and pushed the end of his gun into my mouth. I could do nothing. I could not even shout. My head felt empty. I knew I was going to die. He and his men said many things, some of which I cannot remember because I was so terrified. But I remember him saying that if we oppose Museveni, we are going to die. One of the soldiers said that if my family had never had a funeral, now they were going to have one. I recall being dragged onto the military pick-up truck. I was driven to Rukungiri and taken to the police station.
>
> There were lots of people on the streets when we arrived. Word had reached the town that we had been arrested from the rally. People thronged the compound of the police station. It was late evening, so I was put in a police cell. The place stunk of urine and faeces. I could only sit or lie on the floor; there was no furniture in the cell. I did not eat or drink anything. Later in the night a female police officer

---

104   Ndahura was a Captain at the time of this incident. He was promoted to Lt. Colonel later.

came and got me out of the cell and said I could sit in the corridor, which was somewhat cleaner. She gave me an old curtain to cover myself, and at dawn she gave me a small bucket in which to urinate. Before the day shift officers came in, she locked me up again in the smelly cell. At around 10.00 AM I was brought out of the cell and taken to court and charged with abusing the President and spreading lies to incite people to violence. Again there was a big crowd of Besigye supporters at the court, and the news was in the papers that I had been arrested. I was released on police bond. At that time I did not know that I would be arrested almost every week until the end of the campaigns. But I always found some kind police women at the station, who treated me with courtesy and tried to keep me comfortable if I had to spend the night in the cell.

One of those times I was picked up from my house at night. There was a knock on the door, and a uniformed police woman came in. She said they had come to arrest me. Then in a low voice she told me not to resist, as the police officers outside would then beat me and still arrest me anyway. Then in a loud voice she told me to get up and follow her outside. Outside my house were about thirty policemen, some of them armed. I was very frightened. The woman who had ordered me to leave the house kept telling me under her breath to not look around but to simply follow her and keep up the pace. I did what she told me. People who were still out in the street saw me being led away. A crowd gathered and people followed us to the police station. I was put into a cell and locked up for the night. I was let out the following day on a police bond.

It was after that incident that the Elect Kizza Besigye Task Force appointed a lawyer to be on standby in Rukungiri, to bail out its supporters who were perpetually arrested on fictitious charges.[105]

The behaviour of the armed forces particularly during election campaigns went against what Museveni had promised and what the people had come to expect as part of the fundamental change:

> The citizens of our country were terrorized for a long time by the very soldiers who were supposed to protect them: people used to have to run away from their own protectors, but this has now changed. This is surely a fundamental change for those Ugandans who used to have to abandon their houses for fear that rogue soldiers would come to rob and terrorize them. It must be a welcome, fundamental change for those Ugandans who held their breath every time they encountered a roadblock. Today those traumatic experiences sound like a bad dream, but they were our people's daily experiences before the NRM came in.[106]

It appeared that the brutal regimes of Obote and Amin had un-wittingly provided insulation to future governments against accus-ations of human rights abuses. There was always a worse regime to point to.

In 2005 when Museveni wanted to stay in power beyond two elective terms (four terms in all, including the ten years before the constitution was promulgated), he said a key reason was the need to professionalize the army. It appeared that only he had that capacity. Mugisha Muntu, the longest serving army commander in the UPDF, laughed this off: 'To say that one of the reasons was to professionalize the army – that was merely to gain votes, to make people believe that there was a task still to be done. But he did not do anything about it – I don't think there was ever any serious intention to do that.' Muntu is a bush war veteran, although meeting him you would not have thought he ever held a gun. He smiles easily and has an infectious

105   Interview with Rhoda Mirembe, April 2009
106   Yoweri K. Museveni, 'Was It Fundamental Change?' *What Is Africa's Problem?* (Minnesota University Press, 2000).

laugh. He has an engaging manner and is as comfortable discussing his faith in God as his interest in leadership. There must be a side of him that I did not see, as it was unlikely that he remained Army Commander for eight years on account of his pleasant manner.

It would have been possible for the army to become professionalized – the army taking on the role of protecting the country against external aggression and leaving the internal matters to the police. That could have been done by strengthening the police so that it could be responsible for internal security. There is no reason why the army would still be involved in internal security after all these years. That was understandable in the first years. At first the police was inadequate – but as the economy improved, the police should have been boosted. But the army is still there. Why? Because its presence is an advantage to the incumbent. It is a problem of maintaining the army as a political constituency. That influences almost everything that the army does and how it is positioned.

Courtesy *New Vision*
On the night of 16 March 2010, the Kasubi tombs, an important cultural and

UNESCO world heritage site, caught fire under unclear circumstances. Masses of people rushed there to try and put out the fire. The following morning, ahead of President Museveni's visit to the site of the tragedy, soldiers from the Presidential Guard Brigade opened fire on the unarmed people, killing three on the spot.

Courtesy *New Vision*
17 March 2010. A UPDF soldier cocks his gun as civilians take cover at the site of the burnt tombs.

The army's positioning and behaviour became most evident at those times when Museveni's hold onto power was most under threat – in the lead-up to and during elections. While the military might attack prominent targets such as opposition politicians, they also quite often worked on vulnerable and little-known opposition supporters in the villages. For instance on 6th June 2005, Samuel Obwoya, an FDC supporter in Lira, was intercepted by UPDF soldiers on his way to the market. As he pulled out his identity card for identification, the soldiers saw his FDC membership card. Obwoya reported that he was severely beaten and verbally insulted. He was accused of being a 'Besigye spy'. Obwoya was detained in the UPDF barracks for three days. During this time his family and friends had no idea of his whereabouts. Upon his release he reported the case (CF.NO

SD38/23/6/2005) to the Central Police Station in Lira. No action was taken against the soldiers. For people like Obwoya, Museveni's assurances about guns were hollow: 'We are trying to demystify the gun so that the people can begin to see it as an instrument of security and not of terror. Now the people can become directly involved in the provision of their own security. The days of terrorizing people with the gun are gone.'[107]

The army has also been involved in ransacking opposition party offices and dispersing peaceful assemblies violently. On 6 August 2006, a day before the official launch of the FDC Gulu office, armed people attacked the office and vandalised property. They destroyed registration books, record books, and a photocopier. The following day an FDC rally which had been convened in Kaunda Grounds was dispersed by military mambas (heavy military vehicles) said to be from the Fourth Division in Gulu.

While Muntu's scepticism might be brushed aside by Museveni's supporters as predictable sour grapes, a cursory peek into the workings of the armed forces suggests that indeed there was a task to be done, whether or not Museveni planned to do it. While testifying before a commission of enquiry on accusations that he had been involved in the creation of 'ghost soldiers', James Kazini revealed that the army was rather thin on systems and relied heavily on the goodwill of the President.

Kazini should have known, having spent most of his adult life in the military. He was a member of the Uganda National Rescue Front under General Moses Ali until 1984, when he left to join the NRA bush war. He rose through the ranks, becoming a Lieutenant Colonel in 1991, Colonel in 1996, and Brigadier (and Chief of Staff of the UPDF) in 1999. He was the Commander of Operation Safe Haven in the Democratic Republic of Congo when Ugandan and Rwandan armies clashed in DRC (1999–2000), a period during which certain Ugandan individuals and senior military officers were implicated in extensive plundering of Congo natural resources. In 2001 he was promoted to Major General and appointed Commander of the

107   Yoweri Museveni, 'Was It Fundamental Change?' *What Is Africa's problem?* (University of Minnesota Press, 2000).

Army until 2003. In December 2003 he was charged (together with a dozen other officers) in the General Court Martial for the creation and maintenance of ghost soldiers on the army payroll. [108]

Kazini recounted to the Commission of Enquiry how he took office as Chief of Staff:

> When I became the Chief of Staff (COS)… first of all, there was no correct handover, and take over. I just inherited a stamp from Chefe Ali. When I was appointed I came to Bombo [Military Headquarters]. I only found his ADC Lt. Nuwe [Kyepaka], who was seated on his desk. He said, 'Welcome the new COS, here is the stamp.' I got the stamp, went and sat in the chair and started working. No handover report. The duties which I found were actually rubber-stamping documents… we don't know their source or origin… It took me time to understand because I was endorsing things I didn't know about; uniforms, dry rations, fuel, etc.… you are the COS, you just sign without even knowing the background of what is on the vote.

Kazini described an army that did not have a system for keeping track of its guns and soldiers. 'A gun is supposed to have a BN (battalion number) and a serial number recorded. With us it is not the case, we just give out guns like that. For example, all those guns given to the Arrow Group[109], they were just taken from the stores and given out.' Asked to describe the operational systems and accountability, Kazini told of the heavy reliance on the Commander-in-Chief.

---

108   The General Court Martial pronounced Kazini guilty in March 2008 and sentenced him to three years in jail. He appealed the sentence in the Constitutional Court, lost the appeal, and at the time of his death in 2009 had appealed to the Supreme Court. He was hailed for his courage as a soldier and for his loyalty. He died a violent death, allegedly at the hands of his girlfriend, who is on trial for murder.

109   The Arrow Group was a paramilitary group that was hurriedly put together, initially under the Command of Capt. Mike Mukula, to fight the insurgency that had spread form the northern to eastern Uganda. It has not been disbanded.

You know we have been running the Army because of the good politics of the President. Because that is how LDUs [Local Defence Units] come in. You get surprised, where is the army? 'AC, *Fanya LDUs hapa, andika document fanya Bunyoro/Buganda LDU.*' ['Army Commander, get Local Defence Units here, write documents, work on Bunyoro / Buganda Local Defence Units.'] Just like that. The army has been surviving on the goodwill of the President and his good politics, of the people. *Fanya hii, fanya hii.* [Do this, do that.] But where is the standing army? You remember when the RPAs [Rwandan Patriotic Army] went. About 4,000 soldiers deserted at once. We were all here. Nobody said, 'Let us verify strength… these people have gone, they should be counted as AWOL (Absent Without Official Leave), then their numbers will be known.' Can anybody tell us how many RPAs left the army? It is just an imagined number from the press. But you know somebody should have said 'No, I think they have escaped, here are their names – Kalekyezi, Kagame…' There is no record of the RPA who escaped. We should have had it in the data. Nobody had it.

The continued adverse involvement of soldiers in elections is a concern, but now increasingly there are many more people carrying guns than the regular armed forces.

Odo Tayebwa, a political activist from Bushenyi in Western Uganda, described to me how the state was using firearms to influence the political space.

All the subcounty chairpersons have been taken to Kyankwanzi [political school] and trained as cadres for the Movement. When they return, they come in military uniform, and they find guns at the subcounty offices. The certificates they receive authorize them to use guns – in fact the certificates state that these trained subcounty chairpersons are authorized to wear UPDF uniforms; in essence they turn them into military personnel. During functions and election campaigns, they often don their military fatigues, carry guns, and they let it be known that they are fully in support of the Movement. They also wear the military uniforms in the office, or any other places where they want to cow the people.... Every subcounty has an Internal Security Officer. He comes through the village with a book and says he is compiling a list of the FDC agents. People feel intimidated because they have been told that a monthly security report goes to government. Some of these counties have experienced infiltration of insurgents, so in a sense the officer could have a legitimate reason to gather security information. But he uses this excuse to intimidate people. Once villagers hear that their names are going to be sent to the district, or worse still to Kampala, they quickly abandon the opposition. They know that if the security officer were to say that so-and-so has links to insurgents or rebels, it would be impossible for the framed person to prove their innocence. They do not wish to invite trouble to themselves and their families. Some of them have seen how suspected insurgents are treated.

The political school whose graduates now champion the Movement cause in the countryside was established shortly after the NRM came to power. Over the years it has become a source of controversy, with some people now thinking that its primary objective is to train NRM cadres and to impart NRM propaganda, a partisan activity undertaken using public funds. Amanya Mushega was the NRA Chief Political Commissar from 1985 until the end of the bush war, a position he retained when the NRA took over power. He also became the Assistant Minister for Defence. He remained closely associated with political education for sometime even after he had assumed other government responsibilities. If anybody could shed light on the original core values of the NRA/NRM political education programme, that person would be Mushega. He was unequivocal in his defence of the demystification of the gun.

The gun is like a car. First you should know – there is a difference between training people about the use of the gun and its dangers, and arming them. These are two separate things. There is a big difference between having knowledge of the gun and carrying the gun. I think there are too many people carrying the gun in Uganda. Maybe we made a mistake – but we set out to demystify the gun. There were lots of thieves robbing people in homes, [threatening people] at road blocks – those people that would walk through the village telling people, '*Lala chini*' [lie down] under the threat of the gun. The more people know about it, the less mysterious it becomes. Even the one who is using the gun can be more careful – he knows that… they can disarm you. But we should have assessed after some time to see if indeed it [the practice of demystifying the gun] did what we wanted it to do. We should have evaluated to see the merits and the demerits of the programme. If you discover that it does not work, then you change. But if someone is doing it as a cover-up for some other motive…

Mushega left the sentence incomplete, as though to allow me time to imagine other possible motives. When he resumed it was to give me an analogy. He enjoys speaking in parables.

If you set out from Kampala for Kabale, and after exiting the city you see the driver heading for Mityana, you should ask why. [Because the most direct route to Kabale is not through Mityana.] The driver might say, 'Oh, all roads lead to Kabale. We shall get there by passing through Fort Portal, Kasese, Ishaka… [a much longer and more round-about route].' But what if his purpose for taking that route was to deliver you to robbers in Mityana? Or if he wanted to go to Fort Portal himself, and once he gets there, he will abandon you and your plans for Kabale? There is a difference between making an honest mistake and deliberately misleading people. Our weakness has been not evaluating our goals and strategies, to see if things worked as we planned and if they served the purpose for which they were designed. In those days we did not give people [military] uniforms or the right to carry guns. Now the training is being done for other motives. They are creating cronies. They give the impression that only one person can protect the people.[110]

Mushega might have been surprised to hear what Chapaa Karuhanga thought about the NRM's original attempts to demystify the gun. Chapaa was one of the presidential candidates in the 2001 election. Back then he was the Chairman of the little-known National Democrats Forum. There was as much chance of him winning the election as there was of Museveni inviting Obote for tea at State House, but he stayed in the race to the very end. One had to admire someone with that kind of determination. He told me he first met Museveni in 1979 while in exile, and that he found Museveni very convincing. He spent the first few years of the Museveni presidency trying to advise him informally and in confidence, until he realised that Museveni was only interested in entrenching himself while impoverishing Ugandans. It was his opinion that the politicisation programme was always a tool for Museveni to keep a firm grip on power.

'We had religious and traditional institutions in our societies. They were highly valued. They held people together. Then NRM came.' Chapaa dropped his voice and leant forward. His glasses slid down his nose and his eyes held mine for a moment as he continued.

'It came like a tsunami. They started *chaka mchaka* [military drills]. A reverend, a catholic priest, an elder in the village, they were all taken to the political school. They were told to remove their shirts and collars, they were given sticks and commanded to run. They were told to fall down and roll in the mud. And it was a small boy with a gun telling these religious and traditional leaders to roll and jump. Just a small boy. He caused the reverend to take off his clerical collar;

110   Interview with Honourable Amanya Mushega, February 2010.

174

the priest to remove his rosary. Old women with bare chests. Do you know what that was?' Chapaa paused. I said nothing. He raised his voice. 'It was showing the power of the gun!' Chapaa's clenched right fist hit the open palm of his left hand for emphasis. 'Yes! The power of the gun. The manifestation of militarism. Power was transferred. These other former power bases were being shown where the real power now lies. And who is the epitome of that militarism and power of the gun? It is Museveni. So people fear. In the villages people fear. The mass support they talk about is not real support. People will tell you that the man has said he will fight. They say to oppose him is to antagonize him.'

Chapaa has had unpleasant encounters with the men and women in uniform. 'When we started opposing [the regime], the language they used was very violent – "We shall crush them," they said. I was threatened several times. I received threatening calls, people saying I would be killed; I would be crushed if I did not stop talking and opposing the government. I reported it to the police. The calls were traced to State House Entebbe – at that time it was not fully in use. There was a battalion staying in State House.'

Chapaa does not hold out much hope for Uganda with Museveni still in power. 'What happens after an armed group captures power depends on the make-up and the conviction of the leaders. Rawlings [Jerry Rawlings of Ghana] took power by force, but he managed to transform himself into a democratic leader of sorts. He transformed the whole country. So a leader can be determined, and he can achieve a lot for his country, even if he came through force. But Museveni did not go to the bush for the country or for the people. He went for himself.'[111]

The challenge of keeping track of firearms in a country is not unique to Uganda. Virtually all countries which have experienced armed conflict in recent decades are dealing with the threat of firearms in unlicensed civilian hands. Easier access to guns, licit or illicit, leads to more gun-related crime and contributes to political instability particularly in fragile states such as Burundi, Democratic Republic of Congo, Republic of Congo, and Uganda. Firearms move across

111   Interview with Chapaa Karuhanga, November 2009.

borders and can be incredibly difficult to mop up where their demand exists in the communities and where there is an absence of systems to account for weaponry. Not being able to track guns that are held legitimately by the country's armed forces can only compound the problem. There has been a concern that the proliferation of firearms in Uganda has led to an increase in armed violence. In February 2009 Minister of State for Internal Affairs Matia Kasaija confirmed that the government still had problems with tracking its firearms. 'How many firearms are in circulation? Even the Police does not know,' Kasaija informed a regional meeting on the control of small arms and light weapons.[112]

Now with the government arming a myriad of paramilitary groups and intelligence officers at subcounty and other levels, Uganda seems to be throwing fuel on the flames.

So why did the soldiers not go to the barracks after the 1981–1986 liberation war? Why was it necessary to keep the military uniforms and guns in full view, even in Parliament? Why did soldiers not leave politicians to do the politics, ensuring that the army was subject to civilian authority?

'It would have been unrealistic for anyone to expect that shortly after the struggle the army would have been told to go to the barracks,' Mugisha Muntu explained.

> It was supposed to be a transition, but it was mis-managed because of self-interest. If the incumbent had not had the selfish long-term plan to hang onto power, it should have been possible for the army to gradually step back. With time the government should have removed the army from politics, especially in the transition to multiparty politics. It was all along understood that the army was involved in the political process to bring some stability into the body politic, but that this was transitional.
>
> In 2005 when Parliament started discussing the

---

112   *Saturday Vision*, 21 February 2009.

position of the army in politics, I said that there was no need for that debate; in my presentation to the defence committee chaired by Simon Mayende at the time, I said, 'Look, by keeping the army representatives in Parliament, you are putting them in a very complicated position. There will be only two positions in Parliament – the government and the opposition. So what side will the army take? They are supposed to remain strictly nonpartisan.' But they did not listen. So now the army in Parliament usually takes the government position. That is partisan.[113]

Indeed, it would seem that Museveni himself was of the same view before the country moved to political pluralism. In 1999 while responding to Besigye's criticism that the Movement leadership had become 'dishonest, opportunistic, and undemocratic', Museveni said that the army 'practiced a lot of democracy' but that the democracy was internal.

This therefore means that if the army is to come out in public, it must do so rarely and after internal debate. Therefore, the views of the army that should go public should be institutional and not personal views. Some people may ask: Then why do we have army Members of Parliament if we do not want them to take part in controversial issues, Parliament being the centre of controversies? [They] are not in Parliament to engage in public controversies. They are there as the Listening Posts for the army in the world of politicians.

Museveni then added that this situation was 'only tenable in the Movement system of governance because in a multi-party system it would involve the army in partisan politics'.[114] Clearly, there had been a serious change of heart.

Muntu put the tips of his open hands and thumbs together to define

---

113   Interview with Mugisha Muntu, November 2009.
114   The *Monitor*, 15 December 1999.

a closely guarded space. 'I think because the incumbent wanted the army to remain a political constituency for himself. That influenced the way the army has acted over time. I do not know how that can change as long as the incumbent remains interested in entrenching himself in power. In Tanzania they used to have army representation in Parliament when they had a one-party regime. When they changed to multiparty politics, there was no debate – the army went straight back into the barracks. Now if an officer wants to join politics, he or she has to wait till they retire or resign, so that they can engage in partisan politics.'

Tanzania might have been happy, or at least willing to let soldiers retire from the army before they could join politics, but in Uganda things were somewhat different. Soldiers had discovered that they could not leave simply because they now wanted to return to civilian life. There was a reason for it. 'These are officers in the army but not in active service. There are many officers in the army who are not deployed. That is what is called *katebe*,' Muntu explained.[115] 'Some have been in this situation for years: they are not released because there is fear of the political influence they can have [once outside the army]. If they are out there, there is no control over them. But now they are still under military law, and they can be prosecuted under that law for taking positions thought to be critical of the government. There is a strong sense of self-preservation. It is not only in the army but in civilian leadership as well; even within a large cabinet or in the army council you will find only a very few who will voice concerns consistently, to point out what things are going wrong and to express the desire that things should go back on track.'

Dan Mugarura, a bush war veteran, was once arrested and jailed without trial on suspicion of being involved in subversive activities. The state later 'lost interest' in his case, and he was set free. He explained how he came to be in that unenviable position.

> Illegal arrests, safe houses, persecution of legitimate
> political opposition, leaders grabbing property they
> did not lawfully acquire, open theft of public resources,

---

115   *Katebe* is Luganda for a seat on the sidelines. It means the soldier is not deployed.

stolen elections – these have become routine. That is why Museveni does not want any of us who fought in the bush war to leave the army. He knows that we know what the plan was – we were there. We took serious risks, so he cannot claim that we are marginalized on account of not having sacrificed for the country

Mugarura told me an interesting proverb from Western Uganda: *akakeikuru kakumanya kuri okura kakafa.* 'When you are grown up and respectable, you wish that the old lady who knew you well in your youth would die.' As he bellowed out in laughter, Mugarura explained that Museveni hated to be reminded by the war veterans of the ideals they fought for – the 'old women' who knew him then should therefore be silenced to avoid embarrassment.

Chapter 18: We Want Our People to Afford Shoes

'The major problem in this country is that the guardians themselves have to be guarded. We require, at all levels, a leadership that has the moral authority to lead. The leadership cannot have that authority if they are themselves tainted with corruption. I condemn corruption in all its forms and I wish to emphasize here that corruption can only disappear if the leaders are themselves clean. Only then can they exercise that moral authority, and only then will corruption be stamped out.... In the name of our revolution, therefore, I beg our leaders to change their ways.' – Yoweri Museveni[116]

In 2001 when many people were beginning to feel uneasy about Museveni's stay in power, he was quick to dismiss plans for his retirement. 'How can a parent who has given birth to a child abandon it at the age of fifteen when it is still a teenager?'[117] It would seem that in Museveni's mind Uganda was born when he took over power. It was clear that the parent would not be departing any time soon.

On 23 December 2000, amidst the election frenzy, a new and glamorous object had appeared in the sunny Ugandan skies: the new Presidential Gulfstream IV, which had just been bought at a modest price of 16 million pounds sterling. While the urban elite were outraged, the rural peasants remained largely ignorant of the connection between the excesses of the state and their own impoverishment. The country was at that time gripped by the

116   Yoweri K. Museveni, 'Was It a Fundamental Change?' *What Is Africa's Problem?* (University of Minnesota Press, 2000).
117   *Monitor,* 20 January 2001.

incessant fever of electing its leaders, and if the President needed a new set of wings to go around visiting his impoverished peasants, the squabbles of the disgruntled urban elite were not going to stop the fete. There were those who remembered what Museveni told the country in his 29 January 1986 address, when he was being sworn in as President. 'We want our people to afford shoes. The honourable Excellency who is going to the United Nations in executive jets, but has a population at home of 90 percent walking barefoot, is nothing but a pathetic spectacle.'[118] Museveni now owned a presidential jet and would soon acquire a second one.

In June 2005 when talk of constitutional amendments to lift presidential term limits was rife, primary school teachers held countrywide demonstrations. This was despite assurances by President Museveni that teachers' grievances were legitimate and that the government would address them soon. Teachers marched through towns countrywide protesting the USh 10,000 (US$5) pay raise announced by Finance Minister Ezra Suruma during the 2005–2006 budget speech.[119] The government raised salaries for primary school teachers from USh 130,000 to USh 140,000 (US$70) for the 2004–2005 financial year. The teachers dismissed the increment as meaningless and instead demanded that they be paid USh 200,000 (US$100) as promised by the President the year before. In a knee-jerk response, the police moved in on the teachers in some towns, notably in Kabarole, to disperse the peaceful demonstrations with tear gas. In Kabale District Police CID Officer Stephen Barutagira was quoted as saying, 'We have allowed them to demonstrate for only one hour and any teacher who goes beyond that shall be dealt with as a law breaker.'[120] The teachers' placards told a sad story of neglect and disillusionment:

> 'Reduce the number of the MPs and increase our salaries.'

> 'Save us from the Animal Farm.'

---

118   Yoweri K. Museveni, 'Ours Is a Fundamental Change', *What Is Africa's Problem?* (University of Minnesota Press, 2000).
119   *Monitor*, 22 June 2005.
120   *Monitor*, 23 June 2005.

'We need a living wage.'

'Teaching is the mother institution.'

'Being humble does not mean being foolish.'

Indeed, teachers were not foolish. They had figured out that the one thing that mattered most to politicians was winning the next election. Some placards were boldly tapping into this opportunity:

'No salary increase, no *kisanja*[121], no teaching'

'If you do not consider our voices, the opposition will win in 2006.'

'No pay rise, no votes in 2006.'

'No salary increment, no referendum and no votes in 2006.'

'Why do you sideline teachers? You stand to regret if you don't increase our pay.'

In Kasese, some of the placards read:

'Enough is enough; raise our salary.'
'Ugandan teachers have been patient; a promise is a big debt.'

'Lips that lie are bad in the eyes of God.'

In a show of solidarity, the school children in Jinja town joined their teachers in a procession that brought the municipality to a standstill. The teachers peacefully marched on the streets chanting, *'Twenda emitwalo abiri.'* 'We want USh 200,000 per month.) There was an unexpected touch of humour. 'God saw my work and he was impressed,' read one placard, 'then he saw my salary and he wept.'

In September 2009 Museveni managed to convince Parliament to approve the disbursal of USh 3.8 billion (US$2 million) to set

121   *Kisanja* is 'another term' (of office). The same word means dry banana leaves. In this case the constitution was amended to remove term limits on the presidency.

up patriotic clubs in secondary schools, as well as USh 6.5 billion (US$3.4 million) to recruit, pay, and facilitate eighty Assistant Resident District Commissioners (RDCs) in charge of youth programmes. This money would be put directly under the President's Office. Evidently, a new national diagnosis had been made: Uganda was having problems because citizens were not patriotic enough. Some parliamentarians had argued that the money be given to the Ministry of Education to improve learning facilities and teachers' welfare, but this proposal was rejected. Was the ruling party's propaganda programme about to get a fresh boost from the public purse?

It was not hard to understand why most teachers, especially those in rural primary schools, felt a sense of betrayal by the Museveni government. In the honeymoon years of the regime, they had felt valued and respected. Now a primary school teacher's salary was less than a quarter the salary of a presidential political appointee at the district. How had the tables turned? Only two years previously President Museveni had pronounced himself on the issue of remuneration for civil servants, giving the specific example of teachers:

> Ever since 1986, I have been opposed to pay rises for high level political and administrative leaders without linking it to the pay of the junior cadres and the revenue levels of the country. My struggle has been, actually, to raise the pay of the lower cadres (primary teachers, soldiers, health workers) and scientists. Uganda will benefit more by raising the salaries of scientists than of political leaders and administrators.[122]

Teachers must be very creative indeed, if they are managing to pay for housing, transport, food, health care, and clothing for themselves and their families, all at US$100 a month.

In early 2009 the country was plunged into famine, which was especially severe in Eastern Uganda. The famine, like most others before it, had been predictable. The previous year *El Niño* floods

---

122   *Monitor*, 17 April 2007. President Museveni's statement to the press on media freedoms.

had swept through the countryside, washing away crops, homes, and roads. There had been few harvests. It was clear that people were going to have no food and that most rural households with no other sources of income were going to need food aid. In July stories started to appear in the press that entire villages were facing starvation. There were mixed responses; the Minister in charge of disaster preparedness, Prof. Tarsis Kabwegyere, was reported to have said that the *Iteso* (one of the tribes in Eastern Uganda) were lazy, and that is why they had no food. Members of Parliament from the affected areas were enraged, and when they brought up the plight of their constituents to the floor of the House, some of them were openly weeping. There were calls for massive dispatches of food aid, followed by weeks of empty promises and red tape. Finally some food started arriving – what most said was too little, and for some, too late. Malnutrition levels were running above 50 per cent among children, some elderly people had died, and children were abandoning school in droves to dedicate their time to scrounging for food. Civil society groups started raising funds and delivering food supplies as the government inertia continued.

At the height of the food crisis, I ran into Patrick Okiring, one of the PRA suspects. He was still trying to find his legs in the community, having spent three years in jail on treason charges. He was in Kampala to report to the High Court, a trip he made from Pallisa in Eastern Uganda every two weeks as one of his bail conditions. Okiring traced the origins of the famine to the time when rebellion in the Teso subregion resulted in people being herded into camps.

> In Teso this famine has struck a region that was already on its knees. You have heard of the 1989 Mukura massacre, where villagers were crammed into train wagons by soldiers, the wagons were sealed, and then set on fire – and the people perished in there. The army started to herd people into camps, where they experienced untold suffering. There were many social problems and extreme economic hardships. Children died in big numbers from malnutrition and infectious diseases. People were kept in these camps

to deny the armed rebels bases, information, and food. People are angry, but they are also fearful.

On 12 July 2009, the *New Vision* newspaper reported that the President had 'rushed to Teso' the previous day to make an on-spot assessment of the food shortages in the region. He arrived in Teso in a nine-vehicle convoy, with a fire truck going ahead at every venue to dampen the ground so that there would be no dust. The local leaders took him from one failed garden to another, and scrawny, barefoot children formed part of the crowd as only children can, probably in the hope that there might be some food at the end of the grand tour.

The president gave the people some assurances: 'Don't panic, the people will not die of hunger because crops have failed. We have solutions because we are a government that knows how to handle people's problems. I went to the bush with only 27 people and defeated a whole army. So how can I fail to protect my people from hunger when I'm controlling the whole government? The Government will reallocate the money available to solve the food shortage problem.'[123]

The President blamed the erratic weather conditions on environmental degradation. At one of the places where Museveni stopped to address people, members of the Bukedea Youth Yellow Brigade, their thin chests and faces painted in yellow, the ruling party colour, danced and carried a life-size mannequin of the President. It was reported that during the visit, some ninety-three young people crossed from FDC to the NRM. 'You are welcome home,' the President told them. 'You had made a mistake to go from the doctor who has got medicine, to some fellows who claim to be doctors when they have never treated anybody!'

One was reminded of Museveni's observation of a quarter century before:

> Of course, 'the drought' is now being blamed. Of course droughts kill crops. It is a mark of civilisation, however, that man is able to tame nature and adapt it

123   *Monitor*, 22 July 2009.

to his own needs... It is an indictment of the present generation of African leaders that 20–25 years after independence half the continent has got to be rescued from starvation by international donations of food. Of course, the medicine for droughts is irrigation to ensure that we do not have to rely on erratic rainy seasons.[124]

Now in 2009, in Museveni's twenty-fourth year of rule, his government was appealing to international agencies to help rescue the people of eastern Uganda from starvation. It seemed that twenty-four years of the NRM government had not changed the food security fortunes, or misfortunes, of the people of Teso. Some would say the Iteso were more food insecure in 2009 than they had been in the late eighties.

Okiring believed the famine was part of a wider problem:

> The social and family relationships are strained because now it is survival for the fittest. So now many people begin to look at Museveni as the provider. They have lost their independence, their initiative. You hear people talking of a project here, another one there. There is NAADs [National Agricultural Advisory Development Services]... they have to cope. But the Iteso know that the animals were not taken by just the Karimojong, and the family structure was destroyed in the camps. [There have been reports that UPDF soldiers, under the guise of providing security in Teso, actually looted cattle and drove them to Kampala, or farther west.] While the initial purpose was to prevent the communities from fomenting rebellion, now it has perpetuated disenfranchisement. So the poverty we are experiencing is commissioned, and even the ordinary man in Teso will tell you this. They were a proud and self-sufficient people. They had ploughs. Now very few can afford two bulls to put together a plough. And if you can't plough, you have no harvest, and you cannot feed your family.[125]

124   Yoweri Museveni, *Selected articles on the Uganda Resistance War*, 1985.
125   Interview with Patrick Okiring, November 2009.

In the same month that Museveni made his emergency visit to reassure the Iteso that help was on its way, a fresh scandal was unfolding in the press. The government had, through some dubious procurement process, imported state-of-the-art Land Cruiser vehicles for Ministers and other top government officials, with engine sizes of 4500cc and above. Some of the vehicles were destined for the President's convoy. Each machine had cost US$117,000, probably a significant portion of all the food aid that had been delivered to the hungry Iteso since the famine started. The vehicle maintenance was doubtless going to cost even more over time. The Uganda Debt Network, a local NGO, threatened to take the government to court over the irregular purchase.

Subsequently schools from around the country started announcing that they might close prematurely because of food shortages. The schools were advised to ration the existing stocks more carefully to avoid hungry students staging strikes. Looking at the excesses of the government officials and the serious impoverishment of millions of Uganda, especially in the rural areas, one could not help but agree with the teachers about the resonance between Uganda and George Orwell's *Animal Farm*. One wondered how the Executive justified even to themselves to use public funds for expensive luxury vehicles when school children were going hungry.

But those in power appear unapologetic about the proportion of the national resources they allocate themselves to be able to live in comfort. Many of them consider their positions to be a form of sacrifice. It is hard for the millions of Ugandans who are excluded from opportunities and services to understand how a leader who has been sacrificing for decades will not let any other people sacrifice. Museveni has explained numerous times what he means by sacrifice:

> My own feeling towards power is that it is the farthest thing from privilege one can experience. It is taxing; it diverts you from your own more lucrative activities… and it exposes the leader to endless risks, especially in a country such as Uganda where politics took a very violent turn. Therefore, being in

power, as far as I am concerned, has been one endless story of sacrifice. Ever since 1966, when I and my comrades started opposing Obote's dictatorship, we have never rested... fighting local battles... involved in a most brutal struggle against Idi Amin... a most horrendous war in the Luwero area; and ever since 1986 we have been engaged in battling against one criminal group after another, as well as coping with the endless intrigues of the unarmed politicians.

To call such a contribution a privilege is an insult. There is a real danger that, if those who perceive being in power as a privilege actually succeed in becoming the dominant force in government, we shall be back to square one.... It may be that in the developed countries, where most issues are already sorted out, it could be a privilege to be in government, but in an underdeveloped country it is, if anything, a tremendous sacrifice.[126]

It started to sound like Orwell's characters speaking in defence of their exclusive access to the best food and accommodation on the farm, while the rest of the animals still lived in their cold stalls and got by on starvation rations.

'Comrades!' he [Squealer] cried. 'You do not imagine, I hope, that we pigs are doing this in a spirit of selfishness and privilege? Many of us actually dislike milk and apples. I dislike them myself. Our sole object in taking these things is to preserve our health. Milk and apples (this has been proved by Science, comrades) contain substances absolutely necessary to the well-being of a pig. We pigs are brainworkers. The whole management and organisation of this farm depend on us. Day and night we are watching over your welfare. It is for your sake that we drink that milk and eat those apples. Do you know what would happen if we pigs failed in

126   Yoweri Kaguta Museveni, *Sowing the Mustard Seed* (London & Basingstoke: Macmillan Publishers Ltd, 1997).

our duty? Jones would come back! Yes, Jones would come back! Surely, comrades,' cried Squealer almost pleadingly, skipping from side to side and whisking his tail, 'surely there is no one among you who wants to see Jones come back?'[127]

Surely Ugandans did not want to see Obote back? And after Obote died, surely Ugandans did not want to return to the dark days of Idi Amin, when soldiers took the law in their own hands? And surely the people in northern Uganda do not want Kony to come back? Because, if he is to be believed, only Museveni has the power to keep these threats at bay.

But again, surely Museveni is only mortal. What will happen when he is no longer here to liberate us and to protect us from all our enemies, real and imagined? I asked this question to John Nagenda, who had indeed hinted at the same concern in one of his Saturday columns.[128]

> I said, 'God forbid if he [Museveni] died – however that came about – we would have a very good chance of going right back to where we were.' Because people are just going to fight to take the stage. It is obvious. Quite apart from the fact that he has been there too long. But I did say he should step aside and do what Nyerere did. He put Mwinyi there, then Mkapa after ten years… but he was the boss. So it would be fantastic if he [Museveni] stepped aside, but if he was still running things from the background. So this is now my mission to keep saying that. It's a fact that if Museveni was not there, there would be a great danger of things getting out of control.

Nagenda has been close to Museveni since before the NRM came to power. He professes an unshakable belief in the good of the

---

127   George Orwell, *Animal Farm* (London, England: Penguin Books Ltd, 1987 edition).

128   John Nagenda, 'Shall the People Speak?' in 'One Man's Week', 9 May 2009.

Movement. He calls himself a Musevenite. I do not know of any other person who does, but then Nagenda is not one to follow the crowd. He is not afraid to offend either – his column in the *Saturday Vision*, 'One Man's Week', is famous – or infamous – for lampooning those that he dislikes or despises. Opposition politicians are often on the receiving end of his literary assaults. He has had Museveni's ear for close to thirty years. So is the subject of his retirement never discussed?

'Even the third term, I was opposed to it,' Nagenda continued. 'And I wrote about it. I said rightly or wrongly people will say, "Yes, there is another African, there for the long haul." So I said for that reason I was against the third term. Now we have a fourth term. It distresses me very much indeed. But I have got to be very careful that I do not to do the Movement an injury.... I never want to find myself in a position where what I write deals the Movement an injury. I don't want it.' So was Nagenda concerned with protecting his privileged position with all the perks that come with it, or was his an inability to imagine a different leadership after three decades of the same point of reference? Were we expecting the monkey to be an impartial judge in a dispute where the forest was in the dock?

Chapter 19: How Did a Straight Line Become a Circle?

'Why have we been so successful in battle? This is because we have followed correct lines in military, political, and organizational matters. In military affairs, we scrupulously ensure equilibrium between our aims and our resources; in political affairs we always support right against wrong; and we rely on the masses, ... Our correct line in organizational affairs ensures the correct handling of, for example, the relationship between the leaders and the led, the handling of secrets, and the solving of problems within the Movement.' – Yoweri Museveni[129]

Mugisha Muntu thinks that the majority of people in government now perceive being in power as a privilege, and that the days of leaders sacrificing their comfort for the country are long gone.

'We wanted to transform the culture of governance. But what happened?' Muntu spreads out his hands palms up in a sign of perplexity.

> When we got in, we were as tempted as those who had been in those positions before. So we had two choices: to succumb, or to withstand the temptation on a sustained basis so that we govern the country on the principles of transparency and zero tolerance to corruption. So if we had withstood, after maybe twenty years we could have established the culture. So even the new ones who did not take part in the

129   Yoweri K. Museveni, 'Who Is Winning the War?' *What Is Africa's Problem?* (University of Minnesota Press, 2000).

struggle would be influenced by the culture they found. But many were tempted, and they collapsed. The balance of power started to tilt in favour of those who could not sustain the commitment. And at a certain time they became the majority, but not just in numbers. The critical factor is the top leader. If the top leader had maintained the direction, the focus, then those who remained steadfast would have stood with the leader, and in, say, twenty years, the culture would have been established. But the leader failed in that ultimate objective.[130]

He paused, maybe to contemplate the tragedy of that failure. I said nothing. He continued. 'He failed. The only question is whether he ever genuinely wanted to lead the country in that direction, especially as far as corruption was concerned. I don't know. But that is what he would say.'

There is a sadness in the way people like Muntu recount what they set out to do, and what they now see around them. John Kazoora, Dan Mugarura, Amanya Mushega – their stories strike a cord with experience of another participant in a different revolution. They all ask the same questions.

As Clover looked down the hillside her eyes filled with tears. If she could have spoken her thoughts, it would have been to say that this was not what they had aimed at when they had set themselves years ago to work for the overthrow of the human race. These scenes of terror and slaughter were not what they had looked forward to on that night when old Major first stirred them to rebellion. If she herself had had any picture of the future, it had been of a society of animals set free from hunger and the whip, all equal, each working according to his capacity, the strong protecting the weak, as she had protected the lost brood of ducklings with her foreleg on the night of Major's speech. Instead - she did not know why – they had come to a

130   Interview with Mugisha Muntu, November 2009.

time when no one dared speak his mind, when fierce, growling dogs roamed everywhere, and when you had to watch your comrades torn to pieces after confessing to shocking crimes. There was no thought of rebellion or disobedience in her mind.[131]

Uganda remains a country committed to perpetual electioneering. It appears that at any one time an election is being planned, conducted, or contested. A successful petition leads to a by-election, and the cycle is repeated all over again. An incredible amount of time and resources are spent on election processes. During Amin's and Obote's regimes, no elections were allowed. The introduction of regular elections was therefore welcomed with great excitement when the NRM came to power. Even when not everybody liked the outcome of a particular election, it was still very liberating for Ugandans to have a chance to decide who their leaders were. Increasingly though, the credibility of elections as a means of choosing a leader of the people's choice seems to have been completely destroyed. Many people feel that this is one of the big betrayals of the Museveni regime. As Anne Mugisha observed, 'Political dialogue has narrowed down to a debate between those who think the war created heroes and those who believe it created villains; those who think it was a just war and those who believe it was an opportunistic war.'

In some respects Uganda is like a patient suffering from chronic osteomyelitis – a serious infection of the bone and marrow. The disease does not resolve quickly, and it often leads to death of part of the bone. When a part of the bone dies, the body begins to treat it as foreign. The immune system that has made continued attempts to heal the bone in the acute phase of the infection now changes tactics. It begins to build some form of barrier to shield the healthy tissues from the rot around the dead bone. If the piece is small, the body might be able to eject it along with the pus that pours out of the wound. Often the piece is sizable, and the body tries to exclude it as best it can, so there are endless cycles of the infection flaring up and the body clamping down on the dead bone and the tissue that

---

131   George Orwell, *Animal Farm* (London, England: Penguin Books Ltd, 1987 edition).

surrounds it, producing copious amounts of pus as the battle rages. Each cycle ends with some temporary relief, and for a short while the wound may look like it is healing. Do not be deceived. Underneath the fragile scar the struggle continues, and in a few short weeks a new cycle begins with more pain, more pus, and more deformity. The only way this unholy mess can be concluded is to take the dead bone out. Ugandans have become masters at the cover-up game: dressing the wound and dispensing pain killers, or expensive antibiotics.

At what point does a liberator become a problem? After how long are the liberated people 'allowed' to think their own thoughts and to choose their own leaders, even if those they choose might not have fought in the liberation war? When can the debt be considered fully paid? If one could put a price on liberation, what would it be? Does that debt end with the generation of the fighters, or could it be passed on to their children, so that in effect there is always a superior class of those who fought, or whose parents fought, and the families of those who 'stayed home and hid under their beds'? How can that class distinction be sustained when in many instances those who did not fight lost their children and their livelihoods as a result of the liberation war? Should they still be paying? Should the civil servants who put up with the dictatorial regimes, ensuring that there was some nucleus around which rehabilitation could jumpstart, still be paying?

Some people believe that back in 1986 Uganda was on the right path and that at some point we started to wander off it. Others think we never were on the right path and that it was a false passage from the beginning. Still others would suggest that there was not just one right path; we were simply on one of a few possible right paths. If there was a right path, a correct line so to say, was there a definite point of departure? Or were there many small departures? If we believe the intrinsic validity of the fundamental change as expressed in the ten-point programme, we are faced with the indisputable fact that there has been a departure, and maybe even a complete reversal.

David Mpanga, as an advocate of the court, has spent years shuttling between the various courtrooms in Kampala city and beyond, as well as countless government offices and magistrates' chambers in pursuit of justice.

'I think the state is a fraud. It is a scam,' Mpanga says.

> It is simply a device – an extension of a very personal agenda. It has no [genuine] institutionalisation whatsoever. It only 'institutionalizes' to the extent that it needs to propagate itself. If one person could do all of the things that he wants done, he would go ahead and do them. In 2001 I got a front row seat in the arena to witness this fraud. The election was part of the farce, done very deliberately to hoodwink – it was part of the process. There were no issues identified as such. There were some slogans, a lot of very base abuse, and naked violence. There was blatant intimidation. Guns were mentioned and displayed. If there wasn't a wider cry for democracy in the world, there would still be no elections in Uganda. People captured power, and they would have gone on [to keep it] like that.

> Most people are completely unaware of the true nature of the state. Most people still think the state is benevolent, institutionalised, and that there might be one or two rotten eggs, but that it is otherwise a state. Yet you would be lucky to find one good apple. Otherwise the [regime] is a personal, rapacious, and very predatory tool. Many people support the state and carry on with the farce unwittingly.

> Those components that seem to function do so only because they are allowed to exist. They exist because the 'state' cannot be run entirely by one person. An example – look at the judiciary. It exists, but see what happened when it looked like it was going to assert its independence. Not only were they intimidated physically, but the judiciary was then very deliberately, almost maliciously, watered down. People who were not even qualified to be High Court Judges were appointed as Supreme Court Judges. How can you take people straight from the Movement Secretariat

and you put them in the Supreme Court as Judges? It would be equally scandalous of you took someone straight from the DP Secretariat to the Supreme Court.

David pauses and laughs. 'Likewise, it would be scandalous if they took someone straight from the FDC Secretariat to the Supreme Court.' At this even more unlikely scenario David has another bout of laughter. 'Yet it has been done with the Movement. Everything of that kind operates at pleasure. So some functions still peter on and might look like they are working, but if attention was turned to them they too would turn to dust. The Parliament turned to dust. To my mind it just illustrates that this whole thing is a sham. With regard to the original ten-point programme, I think that there was no honesty on the part of certain actors. I think that people were duped. The ten-point programme was a con.'

There have been varied responses to the realisation that what the NRM regime preached was radically different from what it practiced. And the difference was not simply a result of an ambitious government biting off much more than it could chew; it was not a difference between good intentions and the size of the available resource envelope. Quite often it was the result of greed and self aggrandisement by those in leadership, at the expense of the millions who are forced to pay taxes they can ill afford. Anne Mugisha described her awakening to this reality during the 2001 election campaigns.

> The thing that really agitates me and the reason I got involved in the struggle - is the disparities. The wide, yawning gap between the rich and the poor, and the refusal of government to acknowledge and try to fix these disparities. Disparities in income, and disparities in lifestyle. That is what touched me, what propelled me, and what keeps me going. And for me that started during the campaigns. Until then I had lived a very sheltered life. I grew up in Nakasero [an upper middle class neighbourhood], went to school in Kitante [an upscale school for the children of the privileged]. I went on to Bweranyangi, Gayaza, to university in

Uganda and the UK – and I had never been to Kisenyi until 2001. I had never visited a slum! Never!

Now, in 2001 after the presidential election was rigged, I decided to join the race for a parliamentary seat. I was quite naïve then – I recall Besigye was quietly amused at the fact that I thought the quality of my manifesto was going to make a difference. I thought, well, I had a good enough manifesto, could speak about it, and people would support me. I had no clue how a person in Kisenyi [a slum] lived and what influences shaped their thoughts. During the presidential elections, we had built cross-party alliances, and we thought that these would hold through the parliamentary election campaigns as well, but they did not. So I had to recruit campaign agents and get down to the ground work. That was when I crossed the line that divides Kampala's suburbs from its slums. If you have never been behind Nakivubo Stadium, you know nothing of urban poverty. If you have never descended into the valleys behind Kamwokya market to visit Kifumbira, or never walked the trail behind Bat Valley down to Makerere, you will never know the cruel poverty that is at the doorsteps of our suburbs. I had never heard of or seen *emyala*. [*Emyala* are huge open sewers that run through most slums, carrying with them everything that gets swept or washed into them – slow moving rivers of stench and waste.] I recall visiting one house in particular; there was an old lady in a tiny house, and the inside was dark. I asked why she did not open the window, and she told me that the sewer ended right outside her window, so over the years the garbage had piled up till it closed and sealed her window! And that was where the old lady lived, right behind Nakivubo Stadium.

I recall another place we went to campaign in Makerere Kivulu. We were moving from door to door. The slum kept going way down into the valley. You know, there is the slum you see, and then there is the slum you don't see – the inner slum within the slum.[132]

Anne stopped talking and brought her gaze from that distant place where the story had taken her, and she rested her eyes on me. 'If you have not done it, Olive, go and visit those places. It changed my life.' Anne's voice broke. It was clear that this was something she felt at a very personal level, something she was very emotional about. She paused for a little while and then resumed.

So we were moving down in these slums to campaign. We came upon a lady whose eight-year-old daughter had just died. The woman was half out of her mind with grief and wailing about the dead child. She recounted how she had struggled to bring up the child and how all that had come to naught. And here we were, looking for votes. I stood there thinking, How can we be thinking of printing more campaign posters while this woman sits here, dejected in her loss with not enough money to take her daughter's body for burial? I had money in my purse for the campaign – it was not my personal money; it had been raised to be used in the campaign. I asked myself, What am I doing here? Looking for votes? I could not bring myself to move on, to leave this lady that I had never met, that I had chanced upon in her hour of grief. In that moment, different as our worlds were, I could relate to her as a woman, as a mother. The rest of that afternoon there was no campaigning; I found myself being drawn into the mourning process, joining her neighbours and relatives as they congregated around her home in the slum to share her loss. Yet out of the slum and back in my world, there was no recognition of this kind of life. How could I take this lady's issues back to the debate? The premature death of a child from preventable illnesses, the kind of poverty that prevents a mother from giving her dead child a

---

132   Interview with Anne Mugisha, April 2009.

dignified burial, the inability of this mother to move her surviving children into a safer, more sanitary environment. The sense of powerlessness.

Anne seemed to be searching my face for answers. I had none. She continued:

> These were the things that mattered to me. Yet the debates out there were so far removed from this reality. Instead of getting more involved, I started to feel alienated from the same people that I was campaigning to represent. Eventually I started to think, Maybe if we had won, I could have done something for those people. So in the opposition there was a strong sense of loss – not for ourselves, but the realisation that we could not help those poor people who had risked their lives to support the campaign for change.
>
> I eventually understood why I could no longer just carry on living an ordinary life in Uganda. I don't know why some people see corruption, nepotism, theft [of public resources] happening next to poverty, disease, and squalor but still go home to a good sleep, while such circumstances trigger a different response in others – a refusal to be silent. It gave me a strong sense of freedom and release to be able to talk about the things I saw. Of course I was enraged that the election was stolen, I was mad that we lost. But in the end I felt that I did not have the right to go to those people to ask for votes. At the time I did not know them. What I should have done was to get to know them – truly know them, before I even thought of representing them.[133]

But how do those who are raised up in privilege get to know a slum dweller? Except perhaps as a lowly employee? Why would they risk their privileged lifestyle to change the fortunes of the slum dweller?

133   Interview with Anne Mugisha, April 2009.

Privilege can be enslaving. It is human that we all try to cling to privilege, even if we might acknowledge in our private thoughts that it is either undeserved, or unjust, or probably both. We put up defences. We make excuses. We lie. We only 'give up' privilege when it has been wrenched from us. That is the position in which I have found many people who still profess to belong to the Movement. It gives them positions of privilege: high-paying jobs, free cars and fuel, and phones paid for by tax payers. It affords them business-class tickets and scholarships for their kids in expensive foreign schools and universities. There is free health care when everybody else is paying for themselves (the state having abandoned everything 'public' – public health, public sanitation, public roads, and public education).[134]

But there is another class: those who do not benefit directly from the Movement corruption machinery, who probably detest the rot in the system, but who do not want to rock the boat. They will do everything to distance themselves from the political opposition and will protest vehemently if someone suggests that they are sympathetic to the opposition. They will not risk their livelihoods to oppose even the most extreme government position, as long as the regime leaves them alone to run their profitable enterprises. In fact they are important for the propagation of the regime because the regime relies on them to do precisely that – nothing.

Then there are those who seem to genuinely think they can do nothing. They see involvement in politics as an extremist activity likely to amount to nothing. It is these groups of people that Nazi concentration camp survivor Primo Levi talked about. 'Monsters exist,' Levi said. 'But they are too few in number to be truly dangerous. More dangerous are... the functionaries ready to believe and to act without asking questions.' The NRM government has no shortage of such functionaries. A picture comes to mind: a man stands by a spring with a full bottle of water in his hand. He sees the spring water being fouled but he does nothing; after all, he has a full bottle. His

---

134   Uganda introduced Universal Primary Education several years ago. As with many other government programs, massive corruption has frustrated the program.

troublesome neighbour – the opposition politician, the journalist, or the woman from the north – has no water, so it is his or her problem if the spring water is spoilt. He does not think ahead to the time – probably a few hours away – when his own bottle will be empty and in need of a refill.

In prefacing Franz Fanon's classic, *The Wretched of the Earth*, in which Fanon advocates the use of violence by Africans against their European colonisers, Jean-Paul Sartre wrote,

> When it is desirable that the morality of the nation and the army should be protected by the rigors of the law, it is not right that the former should systematically demoralise the latter, … It is not right, my fellow-countrymen, you who know very well all the crimes committed in our name, it's not at all right that you do not breathe a word about them to anyone, not even to your own soul, for fear of having to stand in judgment of yourself. I am willing to believe that at the beginning you did not realise what was happening; later, you doubted whether such things could be true; but now you know, and still you hold your tongues. Eight years of silence; what degradation! And your silence is all to no avail; today, the blinding sun of torture is at its zenith; it lights up the whole country. Under that merciless glare, there is not a laugh that does not ring false, not a face that is not painted to hide fear or anger, not a single action that does not betray our disgust, and our complicity.[135]

It is possible that there are those who truly believe that the Movement government is the best that there is. They believe that any other government would be just as corrupt, just as unjust – or even more so. Some believe that if a government is better than Obote's, or Amin's, then it is doing all right. Some, like John Nagenda, believe that a certain amount of injustice here and there is the price we pay for a 'stable' society: 'Of course I have to admit that in the pursuit of a

135   Franz Fanon. *Wretched of the Earth.* (Grove Press, New York 1963.)

stable situation some innocent people may get hurt.'[136] One wonders, though, at what point is the price too high?

In *Sowing the Mustard Seed* and *What Is Africa's Problem?* and in many other writings on Uganda's search for freedom, Museveni provided a basis for hope and for the belief that peace and stability were not only possible, they had come. The expectations of many Ugandans of my generation were based on the content of these writings. In many ways they provided a guiding light to direct our steps. In the late eighties Ugandans threw themselves into the challenging task of rebuilding their country with impressive zeal and goodwill. Many young people who would have fled the country for greener pastures decided to stay. We were going to be the generation that turned things around; we were going to make a difference. But if we were moving along a straight line, a correct line so to say, why is the landscape beginning to look frighteningly similar to that of decades gone by?

Just like night settling over a village, there is not one moment at which everyone noticed the distortion. Some people light their lamps as soon as the sun dips behind the horizon. Some people do not light their lamps until it is almost too dark to see the next person. So it has been with Museveni.

There will surely be an end. What will it look like? How will it come? It is like a tree that has stood in the centre of the homestead for generations. Periodically the tree casts some seeds into the air. Some germinate; some are eaten by birds. Some seedlings grow; some are uprooted and thrown in the fire. Most people think the tree will live forever. But those old enough can remember when it was young, and they have seen other old trees cut down and turned into firewood.

---

136   Interview with John Nagenda, January 2010.

Annex.
The Evolution and Character of the National Resistance Movement

Kizza Besigye[137]

I have taken keen interest and participated in the political activities on the Ugandan scene since the late '70s. This was during a period of intense jostling to topple and later succeed the Iddi Amin regime. I am therefore, fully aware of the euphoria, excitement and hope with which Ugandans received the Uganda National Liberation Front/Army (UNLF/A).

Ugandans supported the UNLF's stated approach of 'politics of consensus' through the common Front. It was hoped that the new approach to politics would be maintained and Uganda rebuilt from the ruins left by the Amin regime. Unfortunately, instead of nurturing the structures and regulations which bound the Front together, we witnessed a primitive power struggle that resulted into ripping the Front apart to the chagrin of the population. Some of us young people were immediately thrown into serious confusion. We had not belonged to any political party before, and we did not approve of the record and character of the existing parties – UPC and DP.

The re-awakened party enthusiasts immediately regrouped and started off their mordant and pugnacious exchanges from where they had

137   This document was published by the Sunday *Monitor* on 7 November 1999, although Dr. Kizza Besigye maintained that he had written it for internal discussion within the army. Col. Dr. Kizza Besigye is a medical doctor, a former National Political Commissar, a former Historical Member of the National Resistance Council, and was an army representative in the CA.

left off in the 1960s. Spontaneously, many people started talking of belonging to a THIRD FORCE. This force represented those persons who wished to make a fresh start at political organization, with unity and consensus politics as the centre pin. With a few months left to the 1980 elections, the Third Force crystallised into a new political organization – the Uganda Patriotic Movement (UPM).

The population, to a large extent, expressed their appreciation of the ideas and opportunity presented by the young organisation, but was pessimistic regarding its election success. Pessimism was justified, because the new organization simply had no time and resources to organise effectively nationally, and UPC was already positioning itself very loudly and arrogantly to rig elections – and seemed to have what was essential for them to do so successfully.

It may be remembered that there was a very palpable desire in the population that UPM and DP should unite to explore their mutual advantages; especially, on the part of DP an elaborate mass organization, on UPM's part, fresh ideas and blood, and a reasonable anchor in the very important Security and Defence arena. Again there was a sad failure to meet this expectation occasioned by the leaders. The tragedy that followed is well known to most Ugandans.

After the sham 1980 elections, when Paulo Muwanga (RIP), a leader of UPC (and Chairman of the Military Commission) took over all powers of the Electoral Commission, and declared his own election results, there was widespread despondency and tension. While the 'minority' DP Members of Parliament took up the opposition benches in Parliament, the rank and file of the party rapidly united behind the new forces of resistance to struggle against the dictatorial rule.

The Popular Resistance Army (PRA and later, NRA) led by Yoweri Museveni which started with about 30 fighters, was overwhelmed by people seeking to join their ranks. Within the Buganda region there were other fighting groups like the Uganda Freedom Movement (UFM) led by Andrew Kayiira (RIP), the Federal Democratic Movement (FEDEMO) led by Dr. Lwanga and Nkwanga (RIP), even others largely unheard of like Vumbra Armed Forces of Maj. Kakooza Mutale.

Some of these groups were actively engaged in undermining other fighting groups especially NRA which they sought to project as an army of Banyankole/Banyarwanda which should go back to Ankole. The response of the civilian population was again instructive: they called on the groups to unite and work together, and when they failed, they identified the group which was serious and advocating for unity (i.e. NRA) and vigorously supported it in total neglect of the venomous campaign rife in the air.

The NRM was born as a political organization in June 1981. It was created by a protocol that effected the merger of Uganda Freedom Fighters, UFF, (led by late Prof. Y. K. Lule) and Museveni's PRA. The armed wing of the organization became the National Resistance Army (NRA).

The NRM political program was initially based on seven points which were later increased to become the well known Ten-Point Programme. The basic consideration in drawing up the program was that it should form the basis for a broad national coalition of democratic, political, and social forces. A national coalition was considered to be of critical importance in establishing total peace and security, and optimally moving the country forward. The political program was, therefore, referred to as a minimum program around which different political forces in Uganda could unite for rehabilitation and recovery of the country. It was recognized that there existed many other issues on which the various forces were not in agreement, and that these issues would remain outside the minimum program. To achieve unity, it was envisaged that the minimum programme would be implemented by a broad based government. It was considered important that all Ugandans are able to see themselves in the NRM (as in a mirror).

After the bush war, discussions were undertaken with the various political forces to establish a broad-based government that would reflect national consensus. The NRM set up a committee led by Eriya Kategaya (then Chairman of the NRM Political and Diplomatic Committee) for the purpose of engaging various groups in these discussions. This exercise was, however, never taken to its logical conclusion. Some party leaders blamed collapse of these negotiations on the NRM, but I believe their own internal weaknesses may have been more to blame. It would appear that once the leaders of the political parties were given 'good' posts in the NRM government, their enthusiasm for the discussions waned, and the process eventually fizzled out.

In spite of the lack of a proper modus operandi, the initial NRM government (executive branch) was impressively broad-based. The proclamation which set up the legal basis for the NRM government (Legal Notice No. 1 of 1986) provided for the expansion of the supreme body the National Resistance Council (NRC) to include representatives of political forces or groups. The NRC was subsequently expanded in 1989, and I think all shades of political opinion were reflected in its composition.

From the early days, elections for political offices under the NRM (i.e. local governments) were organized on the basis of individual candidates' merit rather than on political affiliation basis. This approach was overwhelmingly popular because the population saw it as a way of getting good leaders (who would serve their interests and were directly accountable to them) but equally importantly, as a way to avoid reopening of the wounds that had been occasioned by past political activities. Indeed through these elections reconciliation and healing of the society was evident. The executive offices were always filled with due consideration of the whole social structure of the area. Consensus politics conducted through elections based on individual merit and formation of the broad-based government became the hallmark of the NRM.

However, the popular concept of the broad-based government, which had also received support of most political groups, was progressively undermined. It ought to be remembered that due to the support and cooperation of other political groups, no legal restrictions were imposed on political parties until August 11, 1992 when the NRC made a resolution on Political Parties activities in the interim period.

In my opinion, there were three factors responsible for undermining and later destroying the NRM cardinal principle of broad-basedness, especially in appointments to the Executive.

1. The NRM had set itself to serve for a period of four years as an interim government, and then return power to the people. However, it was not very clear how this would happen at the end of the four years. Some politicians in NRM Government who came from other political parties set out to use their advantaged positions to, on the one hand, undermine the NRM, and on the other, strengthen themselves in preparation for the post-NRM political period. Consequently, they fell out with the NRM leadership, and a number of them were arrested and charged with treason.

2. Historical NRM politicians who thought that they were not 'appropriately' placed in government, blamed this on the large number of 'non-NRM' people in high up places, and set out to campaign against that situation. They created a distinction between government leaders as 'NRM' and 'broad-based'. If you were referred to as 'broad-based', it was another way of saying that you were undeserving of your post, or that you were possibly an enemy agent ('5th Columnist').

3. After some years of NRM rule, some in the leadership began to feel that there was sufficient grassroots support for the NRM, such that one could 'off-load' the 'broad-based' elements in government at no political cost.

These factors were at the centre of an unprincipled power struggle which was mostly covert and hence could not be resolved democratically. It continued to play itself out outside the formal Movement organs, with the result of weakening and eventually losing the concept of consensus politics and broad-basedness. By the time the Constitutional Assembly elections in 1994, the NRM's all encompassing, and broad-based concept remained only in name. For instance, while the CA electoral law clearly stated that candidates would stand on 'individual merit', the NRM Secretariat set up special committees at district level whose task was to recommend 'NRM candidates' for support. Not only did the logistical and administrative machinery of NRM move against the candidates supporting or suspected to be favouring early return to multi-party politics, it even moved against liberal candidates advocating for the initial NRM broad-based concept, and others for no apparent reason.

It ought to be emphasized again here that the CA law was premised on the 'broad-based' and individual merit concepts of the NRM because these were popular. So to provide a 'Movement platform' to certain candidates through the district committees, the NRM Secretariat had to operate secretly. That is why very many people were surprised and confused when some senior NRM leaders declared that 'we have won!', after the CA results were announced. Who had won?

It was clear that there were two systems; one described in the law, and another being practiced. Moreover, the conduct of the CA again exhibited the contradictions between the principles of NRM (and law) and the practice. Whereas the law provided that coming into and participation in the CA would be on 'individual merit' basis the practice was different.

I was quite alarmed when I read a document entitled 'Minutes of a Meeting Between H.E. The President with CA Group held on 25.8.94 at Kisozi.' The copy had been availed to me by my colleague Lt. Col. Serwanga-Lwanga (RIP) who attended the meeting. Present at the meeting were recorded as:

H.E. The President (Chair), Hon. Kategaya, Hon. Bidandi Ssali, Hon. Steven Chebrot. Hon. Argad Didi, Hon. George Kanyeihamba, Hon. Miria Matembe, Mr. Mathias Ngobi, Mr. Sebalu, Lt. Noble Mayombo, Hon. Jotham Tumwesigye, Mr. Aziz Kasujja, Mrs. Beatrice Lagada, Mrs. Faith Mwonda, and Mrs. Margaret Zziwa. The introduction of the meeting reads in part as follows: 'The National Political Commissar introduced this committee as a Constituent Assembly Movement Group which wants to agree on a common position.' The arbitrarily hand picked group went ahead to take positions on major areas of the draft constitution, which we members of the CA (considered as 'NRM supporters') were supposed to support in the CA. It is interesting to note that among the 16 hand-picked members of the group, only six were directly elected to represent constituencies in the CA. The others were presidential nominees and representatives of special groups. One member was not even a CA delegate at all. We strongly resisted this approach, and after intense pushing and shoving, this group was replaced by the 'Movement caucus' under the chairmanship of the National Political Commissar Kategaya!

The Movement caucus acted very much like an organ of a ruling party. All ministers (except Hon. Paul Ssemogerere who later resigned from government), were members. Members were not expected to oppose a position approved by the caucus in the CA. The hand-picked group, and the Movement caucus after it, both undermined the principles of the Movement and the law.

The Constituent Assembly was negatively influenced (deliberately or inadvertently) by the executive appointments. In the middle of the CA proceedings, a cabinet reshuffle saw Speciosa Kazibwe elevated to the Vice Presidency, Kintu Musoke to premier, and several other delegates appointed to ministerial posts. Many others were appointed to be directors of parastatal companies. Moderate voices in government and the CA appeared to have been purged in that process. It is my opinion that after these actions, some CA delegates were taking positions believed to attract the favourable attention of the Executive. Most CA delegates also intended to participate in the elections that would immediately follow the CA. This had two negative effects:

1. Being aware of the previous role of the NRM secretariat in elections, some CA delegates would be compromised to act in such a way as to win the support of the secretariat in the forthcoming elections.

2. Some CA delegates saw themselves as the first beneficiaries of the governmental structures and arrangements that were being constitutionalised. So they took positions which would be favourable to them, and not the common good.

As a result of these influences, the CA progressively became polarized, and its objectivity was diminished especially when dealing with Political Systems.

For example, at the commencement of the CA, every delegate made an opening statement highlighting major views on the draft constitution. Analysis of these statements shows that few delegates supported the immediate introduction of multiparty system while the majority supported the continuation of the 'Movement System' for a transitional period of varying length. The positions expressed were very much in line with views gathered by the Constitutional Commission. The Commission noted in its report (Paragraph 0.46) that consensus on the issue could be attained. This was demonstrated by the statistical analysis of views gathered from RCI to RCV, plus individual and group memorandum. (Reference may be made to the index of sources of people's views pages 351–2.)

It will be seen that nationally, at RCI, 'Movement' supporters were 63.2%, and this percentage decreased progressively as they went to higher RCs until RCV (district councils) where Movement supporters were only 38.9% and multiparty supporters were 52.8%.

Among the individual memoranda, 43.9% supported multi-party system, while 42.1% supported Movement. Among the group memoranda, 45.1% supported Multiparty, while 41.4% supported Movement. It is important to note that these views were gathered at a time when there was no impending election, and therefore no campaigning.

For any person interested in the debate on Political Systems, the recommendations made by the Commission at the end of chapter 8 of the report are essential reading. One of the recommendations is that 'Promulgation of any legislation deemed necessary in the public interest should not impair, or diminish, or in any way negate the essential content of Freedom of Association. Accordingly, the Constitutional Commission proposed the following, as the only limitation on political party activities (in Article 96 of Draft Constitution):

'For the period when the Movement is in existence, political parties shall not endorse, sponsor, offer platform to, or in any way campaign for or against any candidate for Public Office.' The CA under the influences outlined earlier ended up with restrictions contained in the highly contentious article 269 of the Constitution. Other very reasonable proposals which were shot down by the polarized CA (by labelling them multipartyist) were:

The proposal for holding of presidential and parliamentary election at the same time. (Uganda paid about US$ 5 million more in order to have separate elections) and separating the Executive from the Legislature. The NRM of 1986–1995 was based on a structure of committees and councils which were also STATE organs. Elections to these councils and committees was based on individual merit. Formation of executive bodies took onto account the broad-based principle, though this was never properly described.

The character of the Movement gradually changed, and the process of change was not determined democratically. Instead, it was continuously manipulated. Established Movement organs were continuously undermined, and others completely ignored. For example, the National Executive Committee (NEC) of NRM was the organ supposed to be at the centre of initiating and coordinating change in the NRM, yet NEC had not met for more than three years prior to the promulgation of the 1995 constitution – in spite of a requirement for it to meet at least once every three months. Instead covert and arbitrarily constituted groups came into play, e.g. District Election Committees, Special CA group, Movement Political High Command, Movement Caucus, Maj. Kakooza Mutale's group, etc. The Movement created by the CA and completed by Parliament (through Movement Act 1997) was different from the one of 1986–1995. Even though there were changes between 1986–1995, the legal framework remained very much the same.

The Movement Act 1997 created a political organization with structures outside the Governmental structure. For the first time, the Movement is a political organization distinct from government. The only remaining link [being that] it is funded by the government.

Unfortunately, instead of describing the Movement as a political organization, the CA chose to call it s a political system – distinct from 'Multiparty Political System', and other systems that may be thought of later! This was, in my opinion, a grave error.

We even ignored advice given to us through a letter written by President Yoweri Museveni (Chairman NRM and Commander-in-Chief NRA) to the CA-NRM Caucus Delegates, dated June 21, 1995. In the letter, the NRM Chairman said: 'the NRM is not a state but just a political organisation that tries to welcome all Ugandans. It therefore cannot coerce all Ugandans to be loyal to it. Loyalty to NRM is voluntary.'

The reality of the Movement today is that it is a political organization in much the same way as a political party is. Having no membership cards does not make it less so. In fact in the letter of President Museveni referred to above, he further explained: 'Then some people may ask the question: "If NRM could be ready to compete for political office with opposing political forces in future, why not do it now?" Do not support doing it now because it is not the best way of governance and, fortunately, for now the people still agree with us. It is only when the majority of the people change their mind that we have to adjust our position. It would be something imposed on us by circumstances.'

So the NRM/Movement System is convenient, and for the time being, a popular means to political power.

About the Author

Olive Kobusingye is a Ugandan surgeon and injury epidemiologist. She is a graduate of Makerere University, the University of London, and the State University of New York at Albany. She is married and a mother of two daughters. She has lived in the UK, the USA, Kenya, the Republic of Congo, and Zimbabwe. She and her family live in Kampala, Uganda.

Lightning Source UK Ltd.
Milton Keynes UK
10 November 2010

162659UK00002B/2/P